Activities for
Elementary Physical Education

Activities for
Elementary
Physical Education

Alice H. Jackson

Joan Randall

Parker Publishing Company, Inc.   West Nyack, N. Y.

249338

We wish to dedicate this book
to all elementary school children and teachers,
hoping that they will get
the greatest possible benefits
from their physical education classes

"It's Physical Education Time"

Activities for Elementary Physical Education is directed toward experienced elementary school classroom teachers and physical education specialists in order to make it easier for them to help the boys and girls get the best results from their physical education classes. It is written in everyday elementary school classroom language. The instructions for the teacher are clear, direct and brief. The stick figure drawings are used wherever feasible to make the meaning clearer to the teacher. We think the teacher will find the drawings delightful, being both imaginative and to the point and reflecting an understanding of how children think and do.

The practical activities given here are based on our actual teaching and supervisory experiences and have been fully tested and proved of value in providing a well-rounded successful program. Because so many children like to be "It" we have changed the rules of many activities to coincide with how the children like to carry them on at home.

The most effective progression for the natural development and growth of the child is used, considering the fundamental skills involved in each activity, the complexity of the activities, and the amount of time likely to be spent on each of them. Many different experiences should be given each child per week. One way of doing this is to divide the class into teams and have each team do a different activity with a student captain. Then rotate after a short time.

The carefully selected activities go right along with the objectives for both the teacher and the children. They satisfy the needs and interests of elementary school children so that most boys and girls can hardly wait for physical education time.

All methods given in each unit of work have been tried many times and proved to be practical in helping the teacher carry on successful classes. A lot of activity is stressed with the least amount of talking and explaining. That is why the directions for each activity are so short and to the point. Children often like to take part in the planning. In several cases the teacher and children are asked "Can you think of other ways of playing this?"

The evaluation criteria for both the children and the teacher go along with the objectives, and also serve as a summary of the learnings desired from the activities given in each unit. It is our philosophy that physical education classes should be fun and happy, active learning times, providing many chances for each child to grow to his greatest physical, social, mental, and moral capacity. This is an activity book which will help you achieve far greater results from your physical education program.

Alice H. Jackson
Joan Randall

ACKNOWLEDGMENTS

We wish to thank the following people for their help:

Joe and Jane, for keeping faith in us and for giving us the kind of professional help, without which this book would never have been written;

Raymond Magwire, Vermont State Director of Health and Physical Education, who has always gone far beyond the call of duty to help with our many projects;

The many teachers and children who helped, over a period of years, with their suggestions and reactions to many different *Activities for Elementary Physical Education.*

Table of Contents

Part Four — continued

PART ONE

Developing the Program

Children look forward to their physical education classes because they are happy times—they are activity times—they are thinking times. Children like physical education for itself. They like it because it provides activities that they can carry on by themselves, at recesses, at noon, or at home after school. They see how physical education correlates with other school subjects—music, which is actually a very vital part of it; art; social studies; math and reading. In fact, physical education is a very important part of their lives.

Physical education helps them to realize the value of good health, which includes not only being physically fit for everyday life, but also having plenty of sleep, the right foods, and a joyous attitude so that they look forward to the great adventure of each day's living. Besides this, it also helps the children to develop desirable character and social traits, so that they can better fit into the world of today and grow into more responsible citizens in the years to come.

--The Authors

1

A Well-Balanced Program

In developing the program, some suggested time percentages for a well-balanced physical education program are given. These are very flexible, as is further seen under the sections for weekly and daily programs. Each teacher must work out the program that he feels is best fitted for his children, his situation and his equipment.

If the school has an activity period, physical education clubs could be an addition to the regular classes for the intermediate grades. However, the physical education program must not only be well-balanced itself, but it must also be well-balanced with all of the other school activities.

SUGGESTED TIME PERCENTAGES

The following time percentages are given for a well-balanced physical education program:

Physical Fitness	10-15%
Stunts and Tumbling	10-20%
Games and Sports	50-60%
Rhythms	20-30%

These percentages would differ according to the needs of the group and the personality of the teacher.

THE WEEKLY PROGRAM

Try to get activities in from each unit of physical education work each week. As is seen in the following weekly program chart, physical fitness might well be done five to ten minutes each day. This would be a good way to start each class for all grades.

Primary children both like and need a lot of rhythms, so they might do them a short time almost every day, ending with a game, instead of following the chart. By either doing this or by following the chart, the teacher will obtain a varied weekly program.

Intermediate children might do their physical education work as units, depending upon the seasons, instead of exactly following the chart. This might give more continuity to the program. They might also be able to correlate some of their rhythm work with social studies and reading. By either diverting in one of these ways, or by following the chart more closely, over a period of time the teacher will obtain a varied program.

If the teacher plans his classes using the following weekly program chart, he will end up within the proper time percentages and with a well-balanced program. The chart is given here for those who wish to use it.

WEEKLY PROGRAM CHART

PRIMARY GRADES

FALL AND SPRING

←		*Physical Fitness*		→
Games	Rhythms	Stunts or Games	Rhythms	Rhythms or Games

WINTER

←		*Physical Fitness*		→
Rhythms or Games	Stunts and Tumbling	Rhythms	Stunts and Tumbling	Games

(Weekly Program Chart—continues)

INTERMEDIATE GRADES

FALL AND SPRING

←		Physical Fitness		→
Games	Track and Field or Stunts	Games or Rhythms	Ind. and Dual or Track and Field	Games

WINTER

←		Physical Fitness		→
Games	Stunts and Tumbling	Rhythms	Stunts and Tumbling	Games and Rhythms

THE DAILY PROGRAM

Make the physical education daily class period fast-moving and interesting, teaching the skills involved as they come into the activities used. Allow no slackness—insist on each child's best work. Get him to participate to his utmost limit.

Sneakers are a must, both for safety's sake and in order for each child to really do his best. Preferably, slacks or shorts should be worn. Classes should be held outdoors if possible or in a gym. If neither is available, the classroom may be used, being sure to modify the physical education activities for the safety of all.

Make the daily program a varied one, and yet keep to the order of progression in each part of the program. Many different experiences should be given each child per week. One way of doing this is to divide the class into squads or teams, and have each team do a different activity with a student captain. Rotate after a short time.

Really try to help each individual child grow to the best of his ability—physically, socially, mentally, and morally. Correlate with other subjects whenever possible. Remember to evaluate the classes—from the children's viewpoint and from the teacher's.

Have fun, but be sure that the physical education classes are teaching learning situations.

PHYSICAL EDUCATION CLUBS

If the members of a school wish, they could have extra physical education clubs during an activity period. These clubs would be feasible for the intermediate grades, during the school day. They could include seasonal intramurals in sports, individual and dual, and track and field activities; folk and square dance clubs; physical fitness clubs; and leader's or captain's clubs.

This would need to be worked out as a school project, possibly on a rotating basis, since other departments would be having clubs too. Children might rotate from one club to another at the end of every marking period, or every semester. Intermediate grade children usually have many interests and should be able to explore several of them in a year's time, or at least during their intermediate school life.

2

Physical Education Equipment

In the section on physical education equipment, two plans are given for checking the equipment out and in. Two methods of keeping or storing physical education equipment are given. There is also a physical education equipment check list which could be used for either method of keeping the equipment.

Physical education equipment is for use. It doesn't do the children any good to have it neatly stacked in a supply room or kept on a classroom shelf or in a closet. But it must be used in the right manner and in the right place. Discuss and decide on necessary safety rules with the children, and help them try to obey them. For examples: Bats and balls must only be used in certain sections of the playground, and other children mustn't run through that section; horseshoes must be used correctly (it helps to have rubber ones), and jump ropes shouldn't be too near them; a high jump area must be away from a boundary ball game so that the two don't get mixed together. If the children have plenty of room, they are safer than they are in a crowded situation, and if teams are kept reasonably small, they are safer than in a very large group. So, allow the children to use the equipment at recesses if they have a recess, or before school or at noon if possible, as long as they use it correctly. If there is enough space, many different activities can be going on at once, safely. Many children look forward to this extra activity.

PLANS FOR CHECKING EQUIPMENT

Team captains should either take care of the daily checking out and in of equipment that is used for classes, or appoint somebody on their team to do it.

All equipment that is used at any other times during the day should also be checked both out and in. A list should be near the equipment box or shelf. One plan is to have one or two pupils in charge of equipment for a week or a month at a time. If anything is broken they should immediately tell their teacher; if anything is missing they should also immediately tell their teacher, and hunt for and, hopefully, find it. The other plan is to have children sign up on a paper or blackboard when they take out any equipment. When they bring it back they either put a line through their name or write the letter "R" after their name. If the equipment gets broken or lost, they should immediately tell their teacher.

WHERE EQUIPMENT IS KEPT

There are two methods of keeping physical education equipment:

1) It can all be kept in the gym supply room, if the children come to a physical education specialist for all of their physical education classes.
2) Some can be kept in the gym supply room and some in each classroom, if the classroom teacher carries on the physical education classes with or without the help of a specialist.

The following check list could be used for either method:

PHYSICAL EDUCATION EQUIPMENT CHECK LIST

SCHOOL _____   19   —19

GRADE _____   TEACHER _____

In Own Room: *In Gym Supply Room:*

	5" Rubber balls				Blocks-tall
	7" " "				"Potatoes"—2"x2"x4"

(Physical Education Check List—continued)

8½" " "				Indian Clubs
10" " "				Dumb Bells
16" " "				Wands or Sticks
Soccerballs				Ball Pumps
Jr. Footballs		BOOKS		Sets of Rubber Bases
Basketballs		Act. for Elem.		Volleyball Nets
Volleyballs		Phy. Ed.		Poly. Hockey Sets
Softballs		Youth Physical		Pair of High
Poly. Softballs		Fitness-AAHPER State Guides		Jump Standards
Fluffballs				Bamboo Poles
Beachballs				Gym Mats 6'x4'x2"
Bean Bags		PHONOGRAPH		Tetherball Posts
Jump Ropes		RECORDS		and Balls
Hula Hoops				May Poles
Ring Toss Games				Pole Goals
Deck Tennis Rings				Basketball Rings
Horseshoe Sets				and Backboards
Paddle Tennis Pad.				Horizontal Ladder
Bats				Record Player
Balance Beams				Balance Beams
Bowling Games				

3

Evaluation Criteria

The evaluation criteria are given under three headings: *for the primary child K-3; for the intermediate child 4-6;* and *for the teacher.* These are given in such a manner that each person can check himself on how he is doing, not only in physical education but also in his everyday life, for these qualities should carry over and beyond his physical education classes to have a lasting value for each one.

The teacher doesn't need to wait until the end of a unit to mention the evaluation criteria. He can do it informally every day in explaining what different activities are for; in talking about how to act; in urging different ones to try harder; in helping children help each other; in trying to get the children to think; and in making them feel good about themselves.

However, the evaluation criteria could also be brought up in parent-teacher conferences. They could be used as part of the child's report card showing how his physical, character, and social traits are developing. Other evaluations are given for the child and for the teacher at the end of each of the four activity units, having to do especially with that part of the book. Each one would make a good report for the child for that activity unit.

EVALUATION

For the Primary Child (K-3)

Do I try hard in physical education class? Do I have fun? Am I happy?

Am I getting stronger? Can I run farther and faster? Can I throw and catch better? Can I kick a ball better?

Do I remember to play fairly? Am I honest? Am I polite? Can I keep out of fights?

Am I learning what it means to be a good sport?

Will I share with other boys and girls? Will I happily take turns? Will I work and play with others? Do they like me? Do I like them?

If I am captain, am I a good one? Am I a good team member? Do I help others sometimes? Do I know that people are different? Am I nice to people who are different from me?

Am I making friends? Am I a good friend? Am I happy to be "It" only when it is my turn to be?

Do I listen to the music and keep with it? Can I use my imagination without feeling too shy?

Do I follow the safety rules? Do I understand why they are? Am I getting to be responsible? Do I take good care of the physical education equipment?

Do I do physical education at home too?

For the Intermediate Child (4-6)

While I have fun doing the physical fitness exercises and tests, do I realize that they are helping me to get stronger? Is my speed, endurance, coordination and skill improving?

Am I getting better body control? Will I keep trying the activities until I really master them?

Do I get along well with the other boys and girls? Am I happy? Do I try to help others sometimes?

Do I understand about individual differences? Can I help somebody else to feel that he is wanted in the group? Can I make him feel that he belongs? Do I feel that I belong?

Do I know, understand and stick to the rules of the games? Do I play safely and try to help others play safely?

Do I make a good team captain? Do the others like me as captain? Do they like me as a member of their team?

Can I win or lose with good grace? Am I getting to be a good sport?

Am I gaining in all the necessary skills? Do I get the feeling of moving with the music? Do I dare to use my imagination? Am I gaining in self-confidence and poise?

Can I keep my emotions under control? Do I have fun in all of my physical education work?

Am I learning to think things through? Do I do physical education at home? Can I teach others?

For the Teacher

Do I have a joyous attitude toward physical education so that the children look forward to it every day?

Do I remember to give them the body mechanics, skills and organization necessary for what we are going to do in class?

Do I insist upon controlled movement exploration and yet can I give them a lot of liberty within safety rules? Am I helping the children to become better sports?

Can I give individual help quietly without taking over the team captain's duties? Do I sometimes get the children to help others?

Do I explain the activities quickly so that the children can get started quickly? Do I keep rhythms moving quickly so that all children really enjoy them?

Do I have the self-control to let the children settle their own differences at times? Do I always watch out for each child's safety?

Do I take the opportunities to correlate physical education with other subjects whenever possible?

Do I compliment the children enough when they do well?

Do I help the children learn how to take good care of their equipment?

Do I truly enjoy watching the children grow and learn in their physical education classes? Do they know I do?

PART TWO

Basic Ways to Develop a Physically Fit Body

4

Physical Fitness
for Everyday Life

Physical fitness means different things to different people. In its larger sense, it is different for each child, since it *should* mean physical fitness for each child's individual, everyday needs. "Physically fit" means for each child to come into contact with as many experiences as possible to stimulate him to his best physical, social, mental and moral development. Done with vim, vigor and vitality, each of the physical education units helps the child to become physically fit.

In its finer sense, the unit on basic ways to develop a physically fit body should include body mechanics, skills and organization, correctives in a general sense, self-testing physical fitness activities, and various fitness tests.

OBJECTIVES

In order to be physically fit for his own everyday needs, each child must be developing his muscular strength, skills, agility, endurance, reaction time and coordination to the best of his ability.

Body mechanics, skills and organization are important because they provide the basic groundwork necessary for a fast-moving class, including the "language" of physical education.

General correctives help each child to learn how to use his body to his best advantage, correct or improve any body defect if there is one, and learn how to relax both mentally and physically, thus increasing his physical efficiency.

The self-testing physical fitness activities help the children's general physical fitness by building up their endurance, strength, agility, reaction time and coordination. They also help to show the value of relaxation.

The three modified fitness tests are given so that the child, the parents, and the teacher can see where the child stands in regard to these fitness tests.

METHODS

Give the various body mechanics, skills and organization as they need to be used in activities that day. They are also useful in the movement exploration part of the lesson, which is really finding out how much space a person needs in different positions and activities, keeping himself under control at all times, not bothering others, and not showing off. Urge each child to do his best and to be very peppy in a controlled way. Insist on correct form. Sometimes, "Try to do it this way" is valuable. "Try again" and "Put more pep into it this time" usually help.

The correctives are all very good, general exercises as given. Each one helps to strengthen the various part of the body under which it is listed. Do it for so long, or for so many times. Try to get the children to do them at home, too. Thus the whole family may begin to do them!

The same holds true for the self-testing physical fitness activities and modified fitness tests. Use student leaders for each exercise or for a series of exercises. Do them to count; try them with music. They are all fun and can be done either singly or as a series. Do them at home, too. Be enthusiastic!

USING THE STICK FIGURE DRAWINGS

Each drawing with its simple directions shows clearly and briefly exactly how each activity should be done and how the children should look as they are doing it. The drawings save many words of explanation. Children should be doing the exercises—not listening to long drawn-out instructions.

The teacher feels secure using the stick figure drawings, because he can easily understand how to do each exercise. The drawings show the right way, which does the child the most good and is also the safest way.

The teacher can make use of the drawings in various ways, as follow:

1) Give the name of the exercise and the directions that go with it to the entire class and let all the children try it. Pick out several who do it exactly right and have them do it again so that all can see. Then have all try again, giving help where necessary. Have all do it many times, with one of them as leader.

2) Have one or more children see the drawings, help them to get into the right positions, and then have them lead the others.

3) Draw the stick figure on the blackboard, or show it on an overhead projector, so that all can see it. Then explain it and have the class do it with a student leader.

4) Demonstrate the exercise yourself, explaining as you do so. Then have all do it, with a student leader.

Spend only five to ten minutes of a class period on this type of activity.

5

Body Mechanics,
Skills and Organization

This section provides the basic groundwork that is necessary for a fast-moving class (see Figures 5-1 to 5-6), including some of the "language" of physical education (such as, attention, at ease, proper spacing, making straight lines, making single and double circles facing clockwise or counter-clockwise). These are the "How to's" and can be given in three ways:

1) As the teacher plans to use them in activities for that day (for examples: children need to be taught how to run, how to make turns quickly, and how to dodge if they are going to play a running-tag game; how to make circles or lines for a circle or line game; and how to throw, catch or kick for a game using a ball). Each drawing with its simple, clear directions shows exactly how to do each one.

2) In a movement exploration part of a class, some of the "How to's" can be worked in with the other activities. Children also need to be reminded to keep themselves under control at all times, not to bother others, and not to show off. Urge each child to do his best, to be very peppy, but to always try to stay controlled.

3) In a game such as "Start and Stop": The teacher tells the class what he wants them to do when he says "Start" (such as, run, dodge, pivot). When he says "Stop" they come to attention quickly. Try not to be the last one. Some of these activities can be done best as a whole class; others, such as making lines or circles, in groups of six to eight.

Body Mechanics, Skills and Organization.

1. How to stand at attention.

head up

chest up

arms at sides.

feet together - stand tall but relaxed. straight

2. How to stand at ease.

L R

(close up of hands.)

feet apart
hands behind back, holding left thumb in right hand, fingers pointing down.

3. How to get Proper Spacing.

Attention.

Proper spacing is one arm distance between each other.

4. How to Start and Stop quickly.

Start quickly but smoothly.

Stop without falling down - "Give a little" - get proper balance.

5. How to make Turns quickly, in opposite directions.

1-2-3-4 Turn.

To change direction - keep same rhythm going. (Turn inwards, count 1 2 3 4 and be off on 4th. count.)

Keep proper balance. "Give a little."

6. How to Dodge quickly.

Step backwards.

Twist. Turn.

Shift weight quickly.

Step sideways.

Dodge sideways, forward or backwards.

Use arms to help shift weight. Bend knees slightly.

Figure 5-1

Body Mechanics, Skills and Organization.

7. How to Pivot.

One foot moves in all directions.

One foot stays in same spot.

Knees bent.

8. How to count off in 2's 3's 4's running numbers.

1 2 3 4
At attention.
1 2 1 2 1 2
Turn head toward next person as says number.

9. How to make straight lines, standing side by side.

Leader.
Look right toward leader to be sure line is straight.

or look left.

10. How to make straight lines, standing in back of someone.

All child sees is the back of one in front of him.

11. How to make circles; single, facing center.

12. How to make circles; single, facing clockwise.

Figure 5-2

Body Mechanics, Skills and Organization.

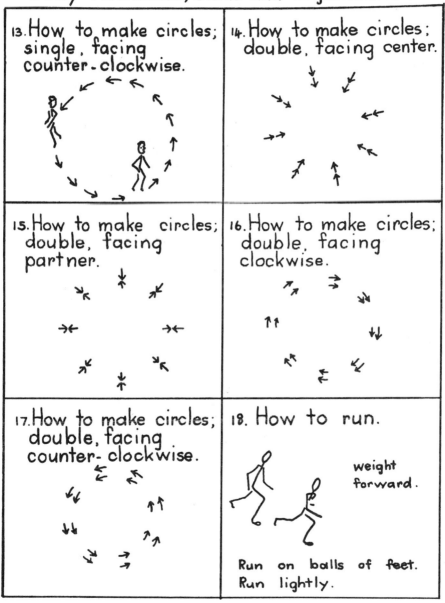

13. How to make circles; single, facing counter-clockwise.	14. How to make circles; double, facing center.
15. How to make circles; double, facing partner.	16. How to make circles; double, facing clockwise.
17. How to make circles; double, facing counter-clockwise.	18. How to run. weight forward. Run on balls of feet. Run lightly.

Figure 5-3

Body Mechanics, Skills and Organization.

19. How to jump from two feet.

Feet together.
Use arms to swing up and through.
Land on balls of feet.

20. How to jump from one foot.

Swing arms up and through.
Land on two feet.
Take off from one foot.
Land on balls of both feet.

21. How to hop.

right foot.   right foot.

Knee slightly bent.
Land lightly on same foot.

22. How to step-hop.

In place or very small steps.

step   hop   step   hop

Step on one foot. then hop on it.
Then step on other foot and hop on it.

23. How to skip.

Lightly.

hop   hop
Step - hop   step.   step

A quick step and a hop- change feet; a step and a hop - change feet...

24. How to leap.

use arms.

right   left

Take off from one foot.
land on other foot.
Land lightly.

Figure 5-4

Body Mechanics, Skills and Organization.

25. How to slide sideways.

③ Close right foot to left.

① Feet together.

② Left foot slides to left.

One foot follows the other, toes pointing straight ahead.

26. How to gallop.

Push with toe.

Right foot ahead.

Close left toe to right heel.

One foot leads with the other following up to it.

27. How to hang.

3 ways.

① Fronts of hands toward body.

② Backs of hands toward body

③ Mixed, one hand one way, one the other.

Arms shoulder distance apart—straight. Feet off ground.

28. How to climb.

Left leg up, right arm up.

Right leg up, left arm up.

29. How to lift.

① ② ③

Use leg muscles.

Bend knees, keeping back straight.
Lift straight up, using leg muscles.

30. How to carry.

Divide weight. half one side, half the other.

Body erect.

Object to be carried, close to body.

Figure 5-5

Body Mechanics, Skills and Organization.

31. How to carry a chair.

Face chair.

Hold seat of chair as near back of chair as possible; close to body.

Walk erect.

32. How to Push and/or pull.

Push off from toes.

T.V.

To pull back, push from balls of feet.

T.V.

Keep center of gravity low. Keep in line with object.

33. How to throw under-hand.

Weight on right foot.

Weight on left foot.

Raise arm back, swing down and then forward. Let go and follow through—weight on opposite leg.

34. How to throw over-hand.

Weight on right foot.

Weight changes to left foot.

Right shoulder back. Bring arm up and back close to ear, throw straight ahead. Follow through.

35. How to catch.

Keep eyes on ball.

Keep in line with ball.

Knees flexed.

Fingers up for high ball. Fingers down for low ball—hands cupped. Wrists close together. "Give" as ball hits hands. Grasp tightly.

36. How to kick a ball.

When kick with right foot—weight is on left.

Keep eye on ball. Kick with instep. Kick either foot.

Figure 5-6

6

Correctives

These exercises are correctives in a general sense (see Figures 6-1 to 6-4). They are good for anybody to do in that they will help the general muscle tone, thus improving the child's posture. They will also help to correct or improve round shoulders, low arches or flat feet, and trunk and legs that need strengthening. The whole class can do them together. (However, in extreme cases of round shoulders, falling arches, or weak trunk or legs, the school nurse should be consulted and the child's parents advised. They might be asked to take him to a physician, who would probably prescribe and explain special exercises to help him. In this case, the teacher's position would be to help to motivate the child to really carry on whatever the physician told him to do.)

Correctives help the children to become and stay physically fit for everyday living by improving their general body posture. Insist on correct form for each exercise, and be sure that all children understand what each one is for. Do them fairly slowly and hold the positions. Work hard and keep the body under control. Do each exercise ten to fifteen times and then relax.

Take the first one from each of the four classifications for a week, with a student leader for each one; the second week take the second one. Continue in this manner.

Correctives _ Round Shoulders.

1. **Stand tall against wall.**

   raise arms above head.

   stretch.

   Stand tall.
   Push body against wall. Stretch.
   Relax.

2. **Head and shoulders circling.**

   Circle 2-3-4.

   slowly.

   Hands behind neck,
   elbows sideways,
   Same other way.

   circle head and shoulders.
   Relax.

3. **Pushing with hands and neck.**

   ① Push-2-3-4.   ② Relax-2-3-4.

   Both hands behind neck, elbows out.

   ① Push both, neck and hands against each other. (4 counts)
   ② Relax

4. **Shrug shoulders.**

   ① Shrug left shoulder up-down 15 times

   ② Right shoulder 15 times.

   ③ Both shoulders 15 times.

   Push shoulders back.   Relax.

5. **Crossed-leg sitting, fling arms to "Y" position.**

   Crossed-leg sitting.

   ① Hands on knees.
   ② Fling arms to "Y" position.
   Push shoulders back.   Relax.

6. **Swing arms forward, down and sideways, and circle.**

   count

   ① Swing arms forward
   ② Down and sideways
   ③ Down, forward and around.
   Relax.

Figure 6-1

Correctives_ Low Arches or Flat Feet.

1. Scrunching and stretching toes. in shoes. scrunch (Shoes off or on.) stretch Do at any time. (Example while eating_ or listening.)	**2. Walking on sides of feet.** walk on outer sides of feet. Walk straight ahead. Keep weight on outer half of feet_ grip with toes. (Shoes off.)
3. Rise slowly on toes. ① ② ③ (Shoes off.) Lower Ready. Rise slowly onto on toes. outer sides of feet. Return to Ready position. Relax.	**4. Foot circling.** (Shoes off.) Support weight with hands. circle upper foot up-out-down and in. Sit with legs crossed_ one knee over other. Change feet.
5. Feet apart, rock forward on toes and back on heels. (Shoes off.) use arms for balance. on heels. Feet apart. on toes Rock forward and back.	**6. Pick up with toes.** Use toes to pick up :- pencil chalk marble (Shoes off.) bath towel.

Figure 6-2

Correctives _ Trunk and Legs.

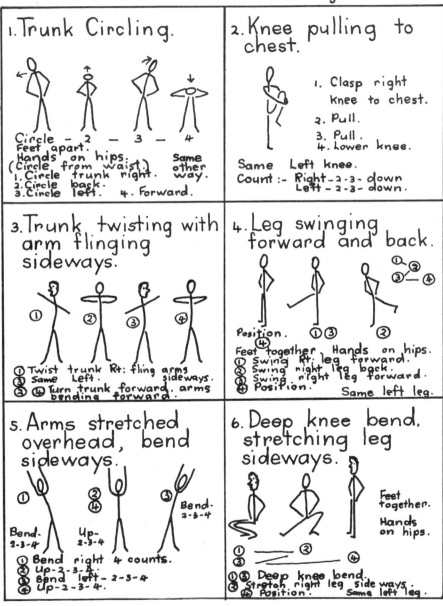

1. Trunk Circling.

Circle - 2 - 3 - 4
Feet apart.
Hands on hips.
(Circle from waist.)   Same
1. Circle trunk right.   other
2. Circle back.   way.
3. Circle left.   4. Forward.

2. Knee pulling to chest.

1. Clasp right knee to chest.
2. Pull.
3. Pull.
4. Lower knee.

Same Left knee.
Count :- Right-2-3- down
         Left - 2-3- down.

3. Trunk twisting with arm flinging sideways.

① Twist trunk Rt: fling arms
② Same Left.   sideways.
③ ④ Turn trunk forward, arms
        bending forward.

4. Leg swinging forward and back.

Position.
Feet together. Hands on hips.
① Swing Rt: leg forward.
② Swing right leg back.
③ Swing right leg forward.
④ Position.   Same left leg.

5. Arms stretched overhead, bend sideways.

Bend.   Up.
2-3-4   2-3-4
① Bend right 4 counts.
② Up-2-3-4.
③ Bend left - 2-3-4
④ Up-2-3-4.

6. Deep knee bend, stretching leg sideways.

Feet together.
Hands on hips.

①③ Deep knee bend.
② Stretch right leg sideways.
④ Position.   Same left leg.

Figure 6-3

Correctives _ General.

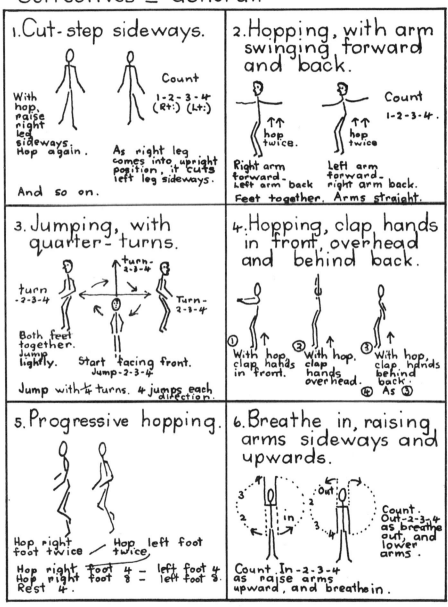

1. Cut-step sideways.

With hop, raise right leg sideways. Hop again.

Count
1-2-3-4
(R+:) (L+:)

As right leg comes into upright position, it cuts left leg sideways.

And so on.

2. Hopping, with arm swinging forward and back.

hop twice.   hop twice.

Count
1-2-3-4.

Right arm forward - Left arm back   Left arm forward - right arm back.

Feet together. Arms straight.

3. Jumping, with quarter-turns.

turn -2-3-4   turn-2-3-4   Turn-2-3-4

Both feet together. Jump lightly.   Start facing front. Jump-2-3-4

Jump with ¼ turns. 4 jumps each direction.

4. Hopping, clap hands in front, overhead and behind back.

① With hop, clap hands in front.   ② With hop, clap hands overhead.   ③ With hop, clap hands behind back. ④ As ③

5. Progressive hopping.

Hop right foot twice.   Hop left foot twice.

Hop right foot 4 — left foot 4. Hop right foot 8 — left foot 8. Rest 4.

6. Breathe in, raising arms sideways and upwards.

3   2   Out   2
2   in   3
4

Count. Out-2-3-4 as breathe out, and lower arms.

Count. In-2-3-4 as raise arms upward, and breathe in.

Figure 6-4

7

Self-Testing
Physical Fitness Activities

These exercises are to help the children build up their physical endurance, strength, agility, reaction time and coordination. They are given here in two series of twelve, though each exercise could be used singly if desired. The body building or conditioning exercises (see Figures 7-1 and 7-2) are for general physical fitness; the conditioning exercises for skiers—both snow and/or water—especially stress trunk and leg strength (see Figures 7-3 and 7-4). Both series are fun, and the children love to see if they can do either one of them without puffing at the end. Each series could be used for a month at a time.

Call the exercises by name. After teaching the exercises, have student leaders, one for each exercise, for a week at a time. Do the exercise to *count* first; then in rhythm to count. After a couple of weeks, try them in rhythm with music, being sure to use a catchy tune. Try to do each exercise six to eight times at first; then increase to twelve to fifteen times.

Relax after each exercise at first; then try to do the complete series without stopping, relaxing only at the end. Take time to build the class up to its physical potential. This would be the exact time when all have been working very hard and successfully, before they have to push themselves too hard to continue. Different children would probably have to stop before others. Watch them carefully. (Ask them to bring in new exercises. Can they make a new routine?)

Body Building and/or Conditioning Exercises.

1. Jumping Jack.

① Jump to feet apart, at SAME time swing arms sideways— upwards and clap hands overhead.
② Feet together — at SAME time bring arms down to sides.

2. Trunk forward with arm swinging.

Trunk forward. Feet apart. Legs straight. Head up. Clenched fists.
① Arms swing forward.
② Swing arms back.
③ Forward   ④ Back.

3. Circle shoulders.

circle shoulder up — back — and down.

Circle right shoulder.
Circle left shoulder.
Circle both.
Push shoulders back.
Relax.

4. Knee bends, quarter, half, full.

Back as straight as possible.

¼ knee bend — hold.
½ knee bend — hold.
Full knee bend — hold.

(Hold position each time.)

5. Windmill.

Feet apart.
Knees straight.
Arms sideways.
① Right hand touching left toe.
② Up straight.
③ Left hand touching right toe.
④ up straight.

6. The whistle one.

Breathe in.
① Raising arms and rising on toes — Breathe in — Hold.
② Lowering arms and heels — whistle as Breathe out.

Whistle out.

Figure 7-1

Body Building and/or Conditioning Exercises.

7. Squat thrust.

① ③

② ④

① Squat _ hands on floor.
② Shoot legs backwards _ body straight.
③ As ①
④ Stand up straight.

8. Fist clenched, arm circling way around.

Start Clench fist.

Circle arm forward - up - back down.

Push shoulders back _ Change arms.   Relax.

9. Bobbing.

①

① Grasp right ankle both hands, pull and relax 4 times.
② Stand and rest _ 4 counts.
③ Same left leg.
④ Stand and rest _ 4 counts.

② ④

Keep back leg straight.

③

10. Deep knee bend with arm circles.

Deep knee bend.
Arms circle.
Knees come up a little as arms go up.

11. Hop twice on right foot touching left toe forward.

Hop right and touch left 1-2.

Hop on left foot and touch right 3-4

① ②

③ ④

Lightly.

① and ②   Weight on right foot, touch ground twice with left toe.
③ and ④   Weight on left foot, touch ground twice with right toe.
(Count.)

12. Shadow boxing.

1 2 3 4 5 6

Boxing position.

Breathe in, hold breath and punch six times.

Relax _ 6 counts.
Continue.

Figure 7-2

Conditioning Exercises for Skiers.

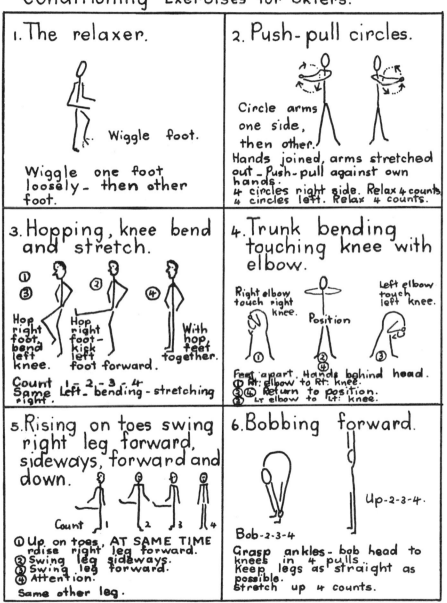

1. The relaxer.

Wiggle foot.

Wiggle one foot loosely - then other foot.

2. Push-pull circles.

Circle arms one side, then other.

Hands joined, arms stretched out - Push-pull against own hands.
4 circles right side. Relax 4 counts.
4 circles left. Relax 4 counts.

3. Hopping, knee bend and stretch.

① ③ Hop right foot, bend left knee.

② Hop right foot, kick left foot forward.

④ With hop feet together.

Count 1 - 2 - 3 - 4
Same Left - bending - stretching right.

4. Trunk bending touching knee with elbow.

Right elbow touch right knee.

Position

Left elbow touch left knee.

① ② ③ ④

Feet apart. Hands behind head.
① Rt. elbow to Rt. knee.
②④ Return to position.
③ Lt. elbow to Lt. knee.

5. Rising on toes swing right leg forward, sideways, forward and down.

Count 1 2 3 4

① Up on toes, AT SAME TIME raise right leg forward.
② Swing leg sideways.
③ Swing leg forward.
④ Attention.
Same other leg.

6. Bobbing forward.

Up-2-3-4.

Bob-2-3-4

Grasp ankles - bob head to knees in 4 pulls.
Keep legs as straight as possible.
Stretch up 4 counts.

Figure 7-3

Conditioning Exercises for Skiers.

7. Leg stretch sideways.

weight on left.
weight on right.

Left-2-3-4.
½ knee bend Lt. leg. other leg stretched sideways. Weight Lt. foot.

Right-2-3-4.

Shift weight to Rt. foot. bend right and stretch left leg sideways.
(Keep shifting.)

8. Leg bending and stretching.

① Right hand on bent right knee. Left hand hold right toe.
② Straighten right leg.
③ Return to ①
④ Attention.   Same left leg.

9. Knee bend and Jacknife.

Starting position - squat down.
① Stretch knees, keeping finger tips on floor.
② Squat down - hands touching floor, outside feet.

10. Hopping, feet apart.

① Hop 6 ins apart
② Hop 12 ins apart
③ Hop 24 ins apart
④ Hop 12 ins apart
⑤ 6 ins apart
⑥ together
⑦⑧ Rest.

Hands on hips - hop feet apart - count 1-2-3-4-5-6-7-8.

11. Trunk twisting touching fingers to toes.

① Touch fingers to right toe.
② Up - arms sideways.
③ Touch fingers to left toe.
④ Up - arms sideways.
Feet apart.

12. Jumping sideways.

Feet together.

Jump sideways to right.

Jump sideways to left.

Figure 7-4

8

Physical Fitness Tests

Three physical fitness tests are given here, two for primary children and one for intermediates, with record charts for each of them. Thus the child, the parents and the teacher can see where the child stands in regard to the physical fitness activities that these tests cover. The following charts for physical fitness tests should go along with the child's folder.

The Triple Posture Test (Figure 8-1) is best for children in grades K-3, and should be done very informally at any time in the classroom or while the class is doing movement exploration. The instructions for standing, walking, and sitting all have to do with correct posture, and help the children look and feel their best. Keep this test in mind, and when necessary, remind a child to stand, walk, or sit "tall."

The Modified Kraus-Weber Physical Fitness Test (Figure 8-2) is also best for children in grades K-3. This test should be given to all in about fifteen minutes twice a year, once in the fall and once in the spring. The parts of the test could also be used as physical fitness exercises to strengthen the part of the body involved. Have each child work with a partner, taking turns on each part of the test. Each one watches his partner and assists him as the teacher directs. All positions, assistance necessary, and muscles being tested are given in the drawings. The teacher will find that sometimes he will need to have a child demonstrate a position so that all will understand. Each child wants to find out two things: Can he do them all and can his partner do them all?

The Triple Posture Test.

1. Standing.

Stand tall.
Head up.
Chest up.
Waist flat.
Knees easy
Feet together.
Hands hanging at sides.

2. Walking.

Stand tall.
Head up.
Chest up.
Waist flat.
Knees easy.
Hands hanging
loosely at sides.
Heels touching ground
first - followed by
rest of foot.
Walk in a straight
line (not pigeon - toed,
nor "duck - walk".)

3. Sitting.

Sit tall.
Head up.
Chest up.
Waist flat.
Press body against
back of seat.
Hands on lap.
Knees bent at
right angles.
Feet flat on floor.

Figure 8-1

The Modified Kraus-Weber Physical Fitness Test.

1. Lying flat on back, with hands behind neck, knees straight, someone holding feet, roll up into sitting position. (Abdominal muscles and the psoas- the big hip flexor muscles.)

2. Same as #1 _ but knees are bent with feet flat on floor, fairly close to body. (Abdominals.)

3. Lying flat on back, with hands behind neck, lift straight legs ten inches.
Hold 10 seconds.

(The psoas muscles.)

4. Lying face down, hands behind head, with legs and lower back held down, raise head and chest off floor.
Hold 10 seconds.
(Upper back muscles.)

5. Lying face down _ face on hands, with shoulders and lower back held down, keeping knees straight, lift legs ten inches.
Hold 10 seconds.
(Lower back muscles.)

6. Standing with heels together and legs straight, touch floor with fingers.
Stay down for count of 3.
(Flexibility.)

Figure 8-2

The Modified Physical Fitness Tests for the intermediate boys and girls (see Figures 8-3 and 8-4) are based on the American Association for Health, Physical Education and Recreation Fitness Tests, and are designed so that the children can see just what percentile they belong in with regard to the seven activities given in the tests compared with other boys and girls in the United States of the same age. They are modified in two respects:

1) The score sheets (also given here) are only part of the official AAHPER Fitness Records, giving only the four main classifications instead of all the steps in between and up to the hundredth percentile.

2) In the method of taking the tests given here, the children can practice them, and be in charge of measuring the distances required, timing themselves, and scoring themselves to see where they stand on the tests, being spot-checked by the teacher in different activities each day. If the children in a class wish to earn the AAPHER Physical Fitness Standard or Merit Emblems, or the Presidential Physical Fitness Award, an adult should be in charge of each event, assisted by the team captain and assistant captain. There are also Special Fitness Awards for the Mentally Retarded and Special Awards for the Physically Handicapped. (For more information, see "Appendix 2.") The level of achievement for the Presidential Physical Fitness Award is very high. Many children will not attain it. Try not to push the children too much.

These tests form a good unit in themselves, or they can be done along with the track and field unit in the spring or fall. The class should be divided into teams of six to eight, each with a captain and an assistant captain. Each team should have, if possible, a copy of the stick figure explanation sheet, and each child should have two copies of the score sheet, one for his folder and one to take home. Then, as the children progress in these activities, they should try to improve their own score. Be sure that all understand each test. Teams should rotate after each child gets several turns at each activity (except for sit-ups; once a day is enough to try that one!). Since children often mark each other harder than many adults do, the results that they get on the tests are probably fairly accurate. Good sportsmanship plays a big part in this, too.

Reading the score sheet is quite easy. If a boy of ten, for example, can do five pull-ups, he circles the number five opposite "ten years" old under pull-ups, and reading to the left, sees that he

Modified Physical Fitness Tests - Explanation.

1. Pull-ups. Boys. Flexible arm hang. Girls.

Arms shoulder width apart.

Pull up until chin is above bar.

Stretch out - Do not touch ground in between.

Lean chest on bar - arms bent.

Head up.

Hang without swinging.

2. Sit-ups.

Lie flat on floor. Hands behind neck.

Sit up and touch left elbow to right knee.

Lie down.

Repeat - using opposite elbow and knee.

Continue.

3. Shuttle run.

30 ft. between marked areas.

Run up and get one block.

Bring back - set in marked area.

Go back and get the other one.

Figure 8-3

Modified Physical Fitness Tests – Explanation.

4. Standing broad jump.

Distance jumped equals nearest part of body to start.

5. 50 yard dash.

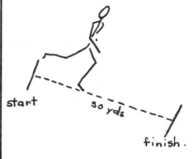

No turns.

6. Softball throw for distance.

Where ball hits the ground counts.

Throw either overhand or underhand.

Child may run up to starting line if he wishes.

7. 600 yard run and walk.

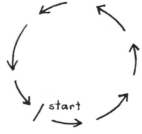

If possible, a 100 yard circle is good for this one.

Go around 6 times.

Figure 8-4

RECORD CHART
FOR PHYSICAL FITNESS TESTS

PHYSICAL EDUCATION   TEACHER: *Kinderg.*_____

STUDENT'S NAME_____   *Grade 1*_____

SCHOOL_____   *Grade 2*_____

*Grade 3*_____

EVENTS	Gr. K		Gr. 1		Gr. 2		Gr. 3	
	F	S	F	S	F	S	F	S
The Triple Posture Test								
1) Standing								
2) Walking								
3) Sitting								
The Modified Kraus-Weber Test								
1) Lying flat on back; sit up								
2) Lying on back with knees bent; sit up								
3) Lying on back, lift legs off floor for 10 seconds								
4) Lying face down, raise head and shoulders off floor for 10 seconds								
5) Lying face down, lift legs off floor for 10 seconds								
6) Standing, legs straight, touch floor with fingers and hold for 3 seconds								

reached the 80th percentile in the test, or Merit Award level. Suppose that he can do forty-one sit-ups. That places him in the 50th percentile, or Standard Award level for that test. In order to be deserving of the Merit Award, he mush reach Merit Award level

MODIFIED PHYSICAL FITNESS
TESTING SCORE SHEET–BOYS

PHYSICAL EDUCATION   TEACHER_____

STUDENT'S NAME_____   SCHOOL_____

Percent-ile	*Years old*	*Pull-Ups*	*Sit-Ups*	*Shuttle Run-30' (Sec)*	*St. Br. Jump*	*50-yd Dash (Sec)*	*Soft ball Throw*	*600 yd Run-Wk (Min-Sec)*
85%	12	6	100	10.6	6'2"	7.0	50 yd	2' 2"
Presi-	11	6	100	10.3	5'10"	7.4	45y 1'	2' 8"
dential Phy. Fit. Award	10	6	100	10.4	5'8"	7.4	40y 2'	2'12"
80%	12	5	100	10.2	6'1"	7.2	48y 1'	2' 5"
Merit Award	11	5	89	10.4	5'9"	7.5	43 yd	2'11"
	10	5	76	10.5	5'8"	7.5	39y 1'	2' 15"
50%	12	2	50	11.0	5'6"	7.8	40 yd	2'21"
Standard Award	11	2	46	11.1	5'2"	8.0	37 yd	2' 27"
	10	2	41	11.2	5'0"	8.2	32 yd	2' 33"
25%	12	0	30	11.6	5'0"	8.3	35y 1'	2' 39"
Need to try more	11	0	26	11.8	4'8"	8.5	31y 1'	2'42"
	10	0	25	12.0	4'6"	8.8	27 yd	2' 49"

or above in all seven tests. He circles the number of what he can do in each test, or, if that number isn't given, then the number next below it, for his age. When he is finished, his Award level for the entire test is the lowest level that he reached in any of the seven tests. He should be motivated to keep practicing the events he is lowest in to strengthen whatever part of his body is involved.

MODIFIED PHYSICAL FITNESS
TESTING SCORE SHEET–GIRLS

PHYSICAL EDUCATION   TEACHER_____

STUDENT'S NAME_____   SCHOOL_____

Percent-ile	Years old	Flexed Arm Hang (Sec)	Sit-Ups	Shuttle Run-30' (Sec)	St. Br. Jump	50-yd Dash (Sec)	Soft-ball Throw	600 yd Run-Wk (Min-Sec)
85%	12	29	50	10.5	5' 9"	7.5	30 yd	2' 24"
Presi-	11	20	50	10.6	5' 8"	7.6	27 yd	2' 24"
dential Phy. Fit Award	10	21	50	10.8	5' 4"	7.5	23y 2'	2' 20"
80%	12	15	50	10.8	5' 8"	7.6	26y 1'	2' 27"
Merit	11	17	50	10.9	5' 6"	7.7	25y 2'	2' 28"
Award	10	18	50	11.0	5' 2"	7.7	23 yd	2' 26"
50%	12	6	32	11.6	5' 0"	8.2	21y 1'	2' 49"
Standard	11	8	30	11.7	4' 10"	8.4	19y 2'	2' 49"
Award	10	7	31	11.9	4' 7"	8.5	16y 2'	2' 48"
25%	12	2	20	12.3	4' 5"	8.9	16y 2'	3' 11"
Need to	11	3	20	12.4	4' 4"	9.0	15y 1'	3' 15"
try more	10	3	20	12.6	4' 2"	9.0	13y 1'	3' 8"

EVALUATION

For the Children

The Triple Posture Test and the Modified Kraus-Weber Test are especially for the primary children. Go over them quickly to see "Can you do this?" Keep a record of what each child can do by checking off activities on his individual record chart. In talking with the parents, be sure to mention them. Ask the children to give the tests to their friends to see if they can do them too. It is also great fun to do them at home with the family.

Correlate physical fitness with good health habits. Is each child getting plenty of sleep, exercise, and good food? Is he having fun growing stronger, and will he stick to these activities until he finally reaches his top notch limit in them? Then, will he keep himself in condition?

The Modified Physical Fitness Tests are for the intermediate children. Have them work on them in teams, with student captains. Let each child see how high a percentile he can make in each activity. Urge them on, but watch out that nobody gets too tired. Remember, each child is different. Be sure that they all understand this, and that each one tries his best—for himself.

As a rule, intermediate children like the corrective and conditioning exercises very much. They have a lot of fun doing them, and it is just instinctive for them to keep going as long as possible.

For the Teacher

Have I remembered to give body mechanics, skills and organization when necessary for the activities for that day? Have I insisted on controlled movement exploration and yet given the children enough liberty so that they have a chance to learn how to control themselves?

Have I had the children do the correctives and conditioning exercises enough so that they get the full value from them? Have I given them a chance to do the Physical Fitness Tests? Do they understand that these tests only test the particular items listed?

Do I give the children chance to gain in strength, and only stop them, if necessary, before they get too tired? Do I show enough enthusiasm for these activities, sometimes even doing them with the class, if possible? (Children love to see if teacher is physically able to do it too!)

PART THREE

Stunts and Tumbling

9

Challenges in Coordination

Both stunts and tumbling are challenges to boys and girls. They like to see if they can do each one in correct form—for so many times, for so long, or for so far. They are fun. They are easy to remember. The children like to try them out on their families. They also like to use them when they are playing school. In fact, they like them so much that they sometimes call them "Stumps and Stumbling!"

The stick figures show very plainly how each stunt is done, and the directions are stated clearly in a few words. An effective, progressive order is followed, by strength and development. Safety hints and precautions are given under methods.

Small, light-weight gym mats should be used for tumbling, for safety. Six feet by four feet by two inches is a good size for elementary school children, since they can move them around themselves. They should be made of some type of washable material. Sneakers are a must, too, since shoes might cause accidents—and also damage the mats.

OBJECTIVES

Each child grows in physical fitness for everyday use by means of stunts and tumbling, because they help him to develop his muscular skills and power, his coordination, and his balance through big muscle activities. This makes him feel good about himself, and helps to build up his self-esteem.

He grows socially because stunts and tumbling give him many chances to grow in cooperation, courage, stick-to-it-tiveness, taking turns, and good sportsmanship. By working in a squad or group, he learns how to become a better member of that group—or a better citizen. He sees that individuals are different, and learns to cope with this difference. He learns how to help others in a nice way.

He grows in learning how to control his emotions. His emotional tone is improving because of his great interest and joy in stunts and tumbling. He is having fun. He is learning how to relax both between classes and at home.

He grows mentally, thinking step by step about how to do each activity. He learns to know, understand, and use the safety rules, both for his own safety and for the safety of others.

METHODS

Keep the instructions and explanations short and clear. Let the children see the stick figures, and read the directions. Have children demonstrate, and have them help each other. Use squad or group leaders, or captains. Sometimes use partners. Be sure that all know what they are supposed to do.

Always remember *safety for all!* See that all safety rules are understood and obeyed. Have plenty of room per child. Keep clear of everyone else. Watch each other. Take turns being an assistant or spotter. Allow absolutely no rough-housing. If anyone is tiring, have him watch the others for a few minutes. Trying to overdo could cause an accident.

Many children like to review the stunts and tumbling from lower grades, by doing them more times, or farther, or longer than before. They are often surprised to find that something that they remember doing easily in the primary grades seems to be much harder for them in the intermediate grades! Assure them their skills will return as they practice.

Divide the children into as many teams as there are mats, each team having a captain. Six to a mat is very good if it is possible. The captain's job is to help the others do the stunt correctly and to keep his team in order. He may either be a demonstrator for his team or he may ask somebody else to demonstrate.

With small children, often half a team can take turns at once. In some of the activities, maybe only two or three at a time can try. As a general rule, use the mats lengthwise for the travelling ones, and sideways for the stationary ones.

PROGRESSIVE LISTS OF STUNTS AND TUMBLING BY GRADE

The progressive lists of stunts and tumbling by grade are given here so that the teacher can see how the activities given for their grade fit in with what the children have had before and what they will have in later years. In starting stunts and tumbling a good rule to follow is to review the activities that the children had the year before, and then work into the new ones. Do not go on to the activities given for higher grades, as many of the children are not physically ready for them. In an ungraded school, increase the distances, or the number of times, or the length of time for the older children.

PROGRESSIVE LIST OF STUNTS, BY GRADE

Kingergarten	*Grade 1*	*Grade 2*	*Grade 3*
Giants	Climb a	Bicycles	Greet the toe
Chickens	ladder	Rabbit hop	Coffee grinder
Birds	Shrugging	Figure eight	Hop and heel
Trotting	shoulders	Heel click	slap
horses	Helicopter	Knee touch	High kick
Jumping	Chinning	Rowing	Minuet bow
Jacks	Swimming	One leg	Stork stand
Ducks	Windmill	balance	Russian bear
Butterflies	Hug knees	Pendulum	in two's
Dwarfs	Sawing wood	swing	Hop-legs
Galloping	Finger touch	Chair	apart
horses	Trees in	Pony stride	Side hop
Blind	wind	Scissors hop	Cart wheel
balance	Crab walk,	Jump, cross	Ankle grasp
Elephants	forward and	feet, and	walk
Rag doll	backward	turn	Human wicket
	Crab walk,		
	sideways		

(Progressive List of Stunts, by Grade—continued)

Grade 4	Grade 5	Grade 6
Bear dance	Double heel	Hand wrestle
Grapevine	click	Stork stand
Hitch kick	Full left turn	Crane fight
Horse hop	Single squat	One knee balance
Thread the	balance	Fish hawk dive
needle	Ankle grasp hop	Wiggle walk
Donkey dive	Wooden man	Kangaroo leap
Hopping, kick	Duck walk	Kneel, jump to
forward and	Rock the boat	feet
back	Rabbit hop	Turk stand
One-half turn	Eskimo hop	Chinese get up
jump	Full squat with	Rocking chair
Knee bend and	arm circles	Acrobatic
jack knife	Scissors	handshake
Double figure	Minuet bow	
eight		
Jump sideways		
Kangaroo hop		

PROGRESSIVE LIST OF TUMBLING (ON MATS), BY GRADE

Kindergarten	Grade 1	Grade 2	Grade 3
Log roll	Seal walk	Inch worm	Bridge
Knee walk	Knee walk,	Knee walk,	Knee dip
Crab walk,	holding one	holding both	Rocking horse,
forward	ankle	ankles	holding feet
Crab walk,	Crab walk,	Rocking horse,	Tip up
backwards	sideways	arms stretched	Forward roll
Stand up,	Mule kick	Wheel barrow	Jack knife
no arms	Egg sit	Human ball	
Log roll,	Shoulder	Rock the	
tuck position	roll	boat	

Grade 4	Grade 5	Grade 6
Jump over leg	Seal slap	Jump the wand
Knee jump	Half lever	Lever
Rocking chair	Tripod	Dead man's fall
Shoulder stand	Head stand	Hand stand
Backward roll	Forward and	Double forward roll
Indian wrestle	backward roll	Forward roll over
(legs)	Through the wand	rolled mat
	(skin the cat)	or blanket

10

Stick Figure Drawings
for Stunts and Tumbling

The stick figure drawings (Figures 10-1 to 10-28) for stunts and tumbling show exactly how each activity should be done. The teacher can clearly and easily see how the children should look in each one. Any other position would need to be corrected. The teacher can feel secure in teaching these activities if he follows the positions and short instructions given in the drawings.

He can teach the entire class with the drawings, using a child to demonstrate as he explains; he can have the captains come up and see the drawings and then help them to demonstrate to the others; or he can show the drawings to the entire class by using a blackboard or overhead projector.

Teach positively. Suppose that a first grader is trying to do the seal walk. The teacher knows just how straight the child's body should be from the illustration. Therefore, he must watch out for dragging knees or sagging stomach, humped hips, or lowered head. But he only mentions these things if a child should get into the wrong position. If a first grader is trying to do the knee walk holding one ankle and is all bent over, the teacher might say, "Try to keep as tall as you can from your knees to the top of your head." Thus the positive hints given with the drawings help the teacher know what to look for in all of these activities.

Good luck-and have fun!

Stunts. Kindergarten.

Figure 10-1

Stunts. Kindergarten.

5. Trotting horses.

High knees.

6. Ducks.

Quack.

Quack

Hands on knees.
Squat way down.

7. Butterflies.

On tip toes.
Slowly move wings
up and down.

8. Dwarfs.

Keep backs straight.
Walk.

Figure 10-2

Stunts - Kindergarten.

9. Galloping horses.

One foot first.

10. Blind balance.

① Heels together.

② Stand up on toes. Close eyes. Hold position 10 seconds.

11. Elephants.

Walk slowly. Swing trunk side to side.

12. Rag doll.

① Position.
② Flop over like rag doll.
③ Put starch (or bones) in legs.
④ Put starch in arms.
⑤ Put starch in back—and head.
⑥ As ①.

Figure 10-3

Tumbling _ (On mats.). Kindergarten.

1. Log roll.

Lie on mat.
Roll slowly over and over.
Stretch.

2. Knee walk.

Walk on both knees.
Body tall.

3. Crab walk.

Straight body.
Move toward feet.

4. Crab walk.

Straight body.
Move toward head.

5. Stand up _ no arms.

① Lie on back.
  Arms crossed over chest.
② Keep arms crossed _
  stand up without touching
  elbows or knees to mat.

6. Log roll _ Tuck position.

① Arms crossed on chest.
  Knees tucked to chest.

② Roll over keeping knees tucked _ arms crossed.

Figure 10-4

Stunts. Grade One

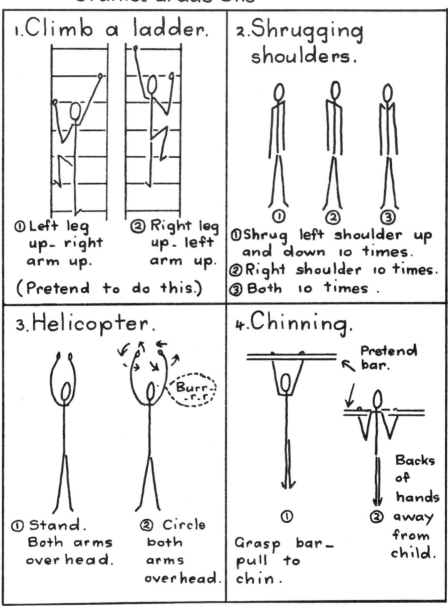

1. Climb a ladder.

① Left leg up. right arm up.

② Right leg up. left arm up.

(Pretend to do this.)

2. Shrugging shoulders.

① ② ③

① Shrug left shoulder up and down 10 times.
② Right shoulder 10 times.
③ Both 10 times.

3. Helicopter.

Burr-.r.r

① Stand. Both arms over head.

② Circle both arms over head.

4. Chinning.

Pretend bar.

① Grasp bar. pull to chin.

② Backs of hands away from child.

Figure 10-5

Stunts. Grade One.

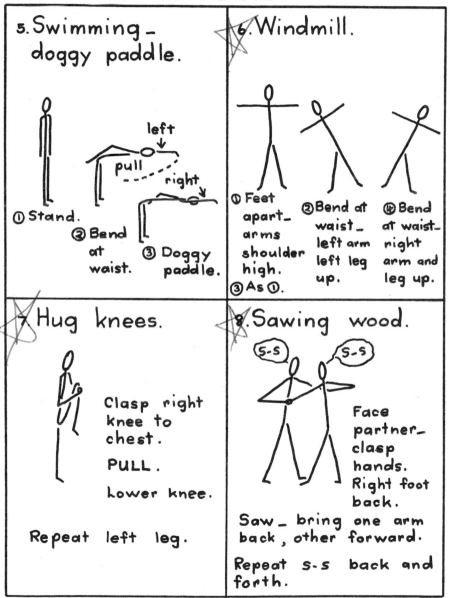

5. Swimming - doggy paddle.

① Stand.

② Bend at waist.

③ Doggy paddle.

left
pull
right

6. Windmill.

① Feet apart - arms shoulder high.
③ As ①.

② Bend at waist - left arm left leg up.

④ Bend at waist - right arm and leg up.

7. Hug knees.

Clasp right knee to chest.

PULL.

Lower knee.

Repeat left leg.

8. Sawing wood.

S-S   S-S

Face partner - clasp hands. Right foot back.

Saw - bring one arm back, other forward.

Repeat s-s back and forth.

Figure 10-6

Stunts . Grade One.

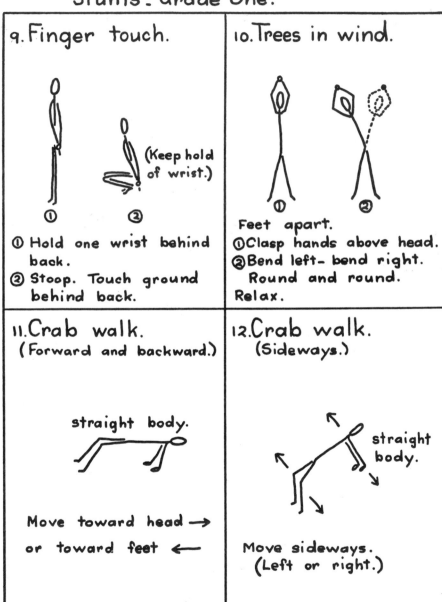

9. Finger touch.

(Keep hold of wrist.)

① ②

① Hold one wrist behind back.
② Stoop. Touch ground behind back.

10. Trees in wind.

① ②

Feet apart.
① Clasp hands above head.
② Bend left- bend right.
  Round and round.
Relax.

11. Crab walk.
  (Forward and backward.)

straight body.

Move toward head →
or toward feet ←

12. Crab walk.
  (Sideways.)

straight body.

Move sideways.
(Left or right.)

Figure 10-7

Tumbling _ (On mats.) _ Grade One.

1. Seal walk.

Keep feet together

Hands point sideways

Straight from shoulders to ankles _ drag legs.

2. Knee walk holding one ankle.

Hold one ankle. Walk one knee after the other.

3. Crab walk going sideways.

Straight body. Move sideways.

4. Mule kick.

① Position.
② Bend forward _ hands on mat.
③ Kick like a mule.

5. Egg sit.

Keep balance.

① Sit. Knees bent Grasp toes.
② Lean back straighten legs and arms.

6. Shoulder roll.

Toes touch mat.

Feet apart. (little way.)

Right shoulder down. Head turn opposite way to shoulder.

Hands on mat. Bend low _ weight on hands. Lower one shoulder _ roll onto it and over.

Figure 10-8

Stunts _ Grade Two.

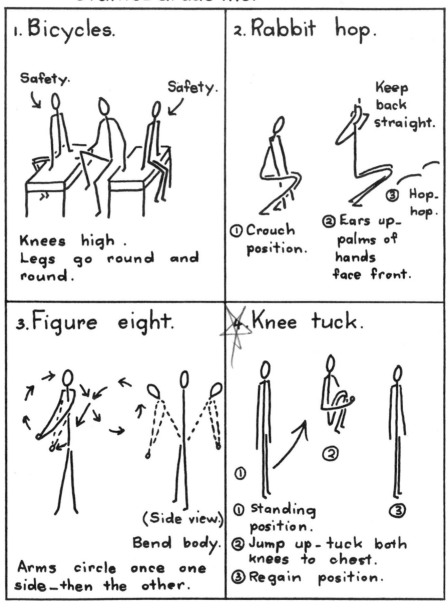

1. Bicycles.

Safety. Safety.

Knees high.
Legs go round and round.

2. Rabbit hop.

Keep back straight.

① Crouch position.

② Ears up _ palms of hands face front.

③ Hop. hop.

3. Figure eight.

(Side view.)
Bend body.
Arms circle once one side _ then the other.

4. Knee tuck.

① Standing position.
② Jump up _ tuck both knees to chest.
③ Regain position.

Figure 10-9

Stunts - Grade Two.

5. Heel click.
(In place.)

② Heels click in air.

① Feet astride.

③ Same as ①.

6. Rowing.

Row forward - Row back - Row forward.

In place.
(Could be done standing. with one foot ahead.)

7. One leg balance.

1.2.3.4.

Knee stiff.

① In place.

② Hold one toe for four counts.

Repeat other leg.

8. Pendulum swing.

Right arm up.

Left arm up.

Right arm back.

Left arm back.

Quickly reverse arms.

(In place.)

Figure 10-10

Stunts. Grade Two.

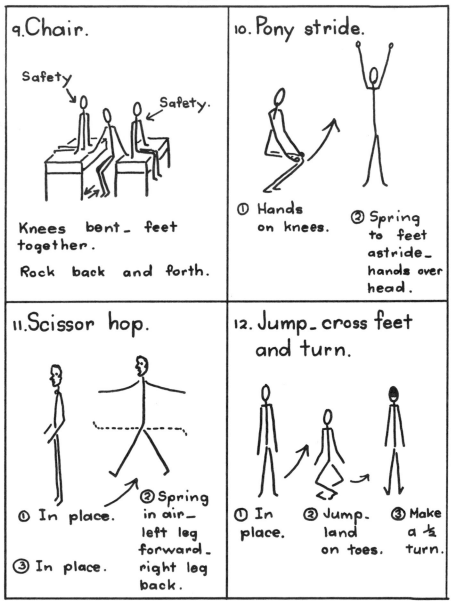

9. Chair.

Safety

Safety.

Knees bent. feet together.

Rock back and forth.

10. Pony stride.

① Hands on knees.

② Spring to feet astride. hands over head.

11. Scissor hop.

① In place.

③ In place.

② Spring in air. left leg forward. right leg back.

12. Jump. cross feet and turn.

① In place.

② Jump. land on toes.

③ Make a ½ turn.

Figure 10-11

Tumbling _ (On mats.)_ Grade Two.

1. Inch worm.

② ③ ④

Walk hands only.

⑤ ⑥ ⑦

Walk feet to hands.   walk hands.

2. Knee walk holding both ankles.

Hold both ankles.

→ Arch back.

Walk on both knees.

3. Rocking horse arms stretched.

① Lie on mat_ face down_ arms above head.

② Arch upper back thus raising arms, head and shoulders. Legs raised _ knees straight. Rock.

4. Wheelbarrow.

#1

#2

#1 grasps knees (or just above) of #2_ walks between legs.

#2 walks on hands.

Let down GENTLY.

5. Human ball.

①

②   ③

① Sit down _ grasp front of ankles.

② Roll toward knee _ then shoulder.

③ Cont: rolling all way round.

6. Rock the boat.

Rock back and forth.

Sit with legs apart _ balls of feet against partner's.

Hands joined.   Rock.

Figure 10-12

Stunts. Grade Three.

1. Greet the toe.

Touch toe to forehead. Hold 5 seconds.

Repeat other foot.

2. Coffee Grinder.

Right. Left.

Back to back. (Half movement.)

Facing partner- hands joined. Boy start right foot- girl left. Turn under boy's left arm- girl's right arm. Turn around and around.

3. Hop and heel slap. (In place.)

② Hop-slap both heels with hands.

① Position.

③ Position.

4. High kick.

up   high   higher

In place.

Kick as high as possible.

Figure 10-13

Stunts - Grade Three.

5. Minuet bow.

① In place.

② Down on one heel, other leg straight.

6. Stork stand.

Eyes closed.

Foot against inside of knee.

Get position.
Close eyes.
Hold 10 seconds.
(Hold without moving.)

7. Russian bear. (In two's.)

Left.   Left.

Change feet with hop.

8. Hop - legs apart.

① ② ③

In place.
① Legs together.
② Legs apart in air.
③ Legs together.

Figure 10-14

Stunts – Grade Three.

9. Side hop.

Both feet together–
hop side to side.

10. Cartwheel.

Position.

Keep head back.
Back arched.

11. Ankle grasp walk.

Grasp ankles.
Stiff knees.

Walk forward.

12. Human wicket.

Position.

Hands touch
floor–
Hold position
5 seconds.

Figure 10-15

Tumbling. (On mats.) Grade Three.

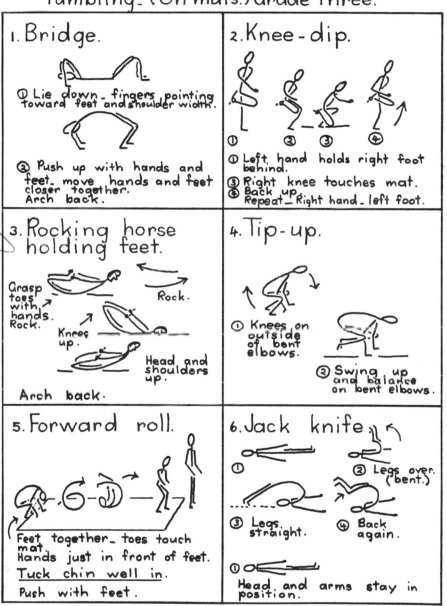

1. Bridge.

① Lie down _ fingers pointing toward feet and shoulder width.

② Push up with hands and feet_ move hands and feet closer together. Arch back.

2. Knee-dip.

①   ②   ③   ④

① Left hand holds right foot behind.
③ Right knee touches mat.
④ Back up.
Repeat_ Right hand _ left foot.

3. Rocking horse holding feet.

Grasp toes with hands. Rock.

Rock.

Knees up.

Head and shoulders up.

Arch back.

4. Tip-up.

① Knees on outside of bent elbows.

② Swing up and balance on bent elbows.

5. Forward roll.

Feet together_ toes touch mat. Hands just in front of feet.
Tuck chin well in.
Push with feet.

6. Jack knife.

①   ② Legs over. ("bent.)

③ Legs straight.   ④ Back again.

①

Head and arms stay in position.

Figure 10-16

Stunts_ Grade Four.

1. Bear dance.

① Right knee bent.   ② Left knee bent.

Change feet quickly.

2. Grapevine.

Hands twine between legs _ around ankles_ and clasp in front.

3. Hitch kick.

① Hop right_ left back.   ② Hop left_ right back.   ③ Hop right_ left front.   ④ Hop left_ right front.

Change feet quickly.

4. Horse hop. (In place.)

① Squat on one heel _ other leg out sideways.   ② With a jump_ quickly change feet.

Figure 10-17

Stunts - Grade Four.

5. Thread the needle.

(Hands joined.)

① Step one foot through joined hands.
② Two legs through.
③ Hands now behind back.
④ Unthread needle. (legs.)

6. Donkey dive.

Arms, body and back leg parallel with floor.

Change feet quickly.

7. Hopping, kick forward and back.

① Hop right leg - at same time kick left forward.
② Hop right - left back. Change feet.
③ Hop left - forward right.
④ Hop left - back right.

8. One-half turn jump. (Left - right.)

Standing left-jump and turn left.

Standing right- jump and turn right.

Land exactly ½ turn around.
Do not move foot as land.

Figure 10-18

Stunts _ Grade Four.

9. Knee bend and jack-knife.

① Knees bend. Hands on floor outside feet.

② Legs straight. Hands on floor outside feet. Jack-knife.

10. Double figure 8.

Circle arms twice each side.

Bend trunk _ circle way down.

(In place.)

11. Jump sideways.

Back and forth.

As jump sideways to left, swing arms to left.

As jump sideways to right, swing arms to right.

(Legs together.)

12. Kangaroo hop.

Hands in front of chest.

Leap lightly.

Figure 10-19

Tumbling _ (On mats.) _ Grade Four.

1. Jump over leg.

① Hold right leg with left hand.

② Jump left leg through loop.

Balance _ release.

2. Knee jump.

① Kneel.

② Swing arms, hard.

③ Feet should land where knees were first.

3. Rocking chair.

Rock back and forth.

Sit on each others' feet, knees bent, hands around shoulders.

4. Shoulder stand.

① Position

② Legs up.

③ Push with hands.

④ Legs straight.

⑤ Bend knees.

⑥ Back to position.

Shoulders stay down. Hands push, and help hold back up.

5. Backward roll.

Sit _ hands on mat.

Bend knees.

Tuck chin well in.

Push with hands and feet.

6. Indian wrestle.

(Legs.)

① Lie down. Join nearest hands.

② Raise nearest leg 3 times.

On 3rd: count, hook knees and try to pull the other one over.

Figure 10-20

Stunts - Grade Five.

1. Double heel click.

① ② ③

① Feet astride.
② Heels click together
   twice, in air.
③ Return to position.
(In place.)

2. Full left turn — and right turn.

No
moving
feet as
land.

Spring — Make one
complete turn.

3. Single squat balance.

① ②

① Position.
② Hold one leg off floor
   for 5 seconds.

4. Ankle grasp hop.

Hold ankles all the
way.

Figure 10-21

Stunts — Grade Five.

5. Wooden Man.

① "A" lie down stiff.
② Three people pick up "A" —
two at shoulders — one
holding feet still <u>on floor</u>.
③ "A" now upright.

6. Duck walk.

Hands on knees.
Squat way down.

7. Rock the boat.

Sit with legs apart —
balls of feet against
partner's.
Hands joined.

Rock back and forth.

8. Rabbit hop.

① Crouch
position.
② Ears up.
Palms face   ③ Hop.
front.   Hop.
Straight back.

Figure 10-22

Stunts. Grade Five.

9. Eskimo hop.

Knees as stiff as possible.
Hop on balls of feet.
Arms circle forward and around as hop.

10. Full squat with arm circles.

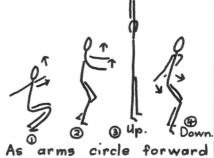

As arms circle forward and up - body stretches up.

(In place. Feet stay on floor.)

11. Scissors.

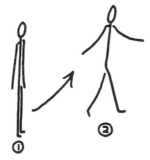

① Position.
② Right leg forward. left leg backward.

(In place.)

12. Minuet bow.

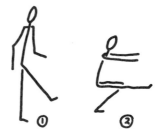

① In place.
② Down on one heel— other leg straight.

Figure 10-23

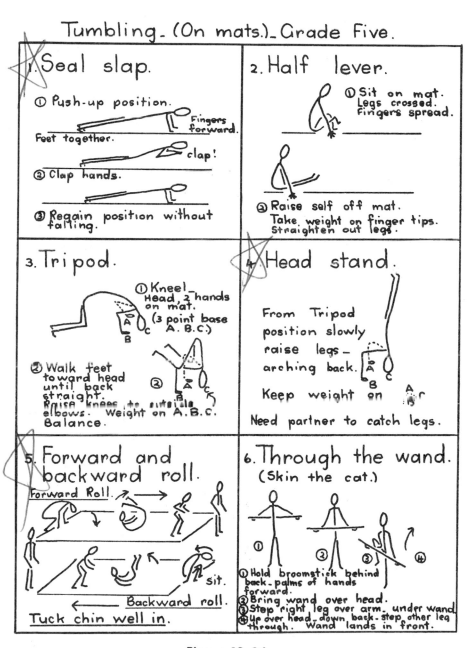

Tumbling. (On mats.) Grade Five.

1. Seal slap.
① Push-up position.
Feet together.
Fingers forward.
② Clap hands.
clap!
③ Regain position without falling.

2. Half lever.
① Sit on mat. Legs crossed. Fingers spread.
② Raise self off mat. Take weight on finger tips. Straighten out legs.

3. Tripod.
① Kneel. Head, 2 hands on mat. (3 point base A. B. C.)
② Walk feet toward head until back straight. Raise knees to outside elbows. Weight on A. B. C. Balance.

4. Head stand.
From Tripod position slowly raise legs - arching back.
Keep weight on A.
Need partner to catch legs.

5. Forward and backward roll.
Forward Roll.
sit.
Backward roll.
Tuck chin well in.

6. Through the wand. (Skin the cat.)
① ② ③ ④
① Hold broomstick behind back. palms of hands forward.
② Bring wand over head.
③ Step right leg over arm. under wand.
④ Up over head - down back - step other leg through. Wand lands in front.

Figure 10-24

Stunts_ Grade Six.

1. Hand wrestle.
(Two ways.)

On two feet
Push or Pull
partner out
of circle.

All feet in a
straight line.
Make opponent
move one
foot.

(Use one hand only.)

2. Stork stand.

Eyes
closed.

Hold position 10
seconds without
moving.

3. Crane fight.
(Two ways.)

Standing on
one foot_ Push
or Pull opponent
out of circle.

(Use one
hand only.)

Standing
on one
foot make
opponent
move his
foot.

4. One knee balance.

① Kneel
on one
knee

② Stretch
other leg
out
straight
behind.
Hold 5 seconds.

Figure 10-25

Stunts. Grade Six.

5. Fish hawk dive.

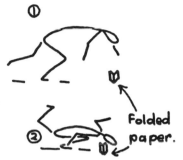

Folded paper.

Pick up folded paper in teeth _ without touching hands or other foot to floor.

6. Wiggle walk.

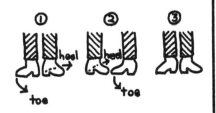

Stand toes apart.

By moving toe of one foot and heel of other _ move sideways.

Repeat using other order.

7. Kangaroo leap.

Sideview.

Front view.

① Crouch down _ hands on floor.
② Shoot legs to side. Legs straight.
③ As ①
④ Shoot legs other side.

8. Kneel _ jump to feet.

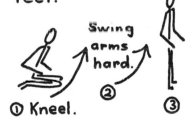

Swing arms hard.

① Kneel.

Swing arms hard. jump from kneeling to standing position.

Figure 10-26

Stunts - Grade Six.

9. Turk stand.

① Cross legs.
② Sit down legs crossed.
③ Stand up again.

(Keep arms folded.)

10. Chinese get up.

① Back to back. Arms hooked.
② Sit down.
③ Stand up.
(Arms hooked all the time.)

11. Rocking chair.

Sit on each others' feet, knees bent, hands around shoulders.

Rock back and forth.

12. Acrobatic handshake.

(Hands joined.)
A lifts right leg over arms.
B lifts left leg over arms.
A lifts left leg over B's back.
B lifts right leg over A's back.

(Make complete turn.)

Figure 10-27

Tumbling _ (On mats.) _ Grade Six.

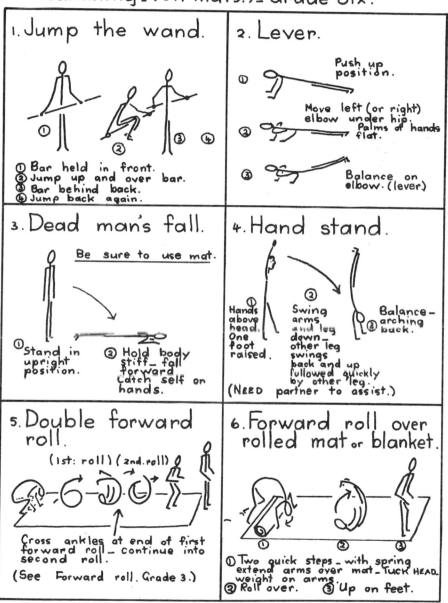

1. Jump the wand.

① Bar held in front.
② Jump up and over bar.
③ Bar behind back.
④ Jump back again.

2. Lever.

Push up position.

Move left (or right) elbow under hip.
Palms of hands flat.

Balance on elbow. (lever.)

3. Dead man's fall.

Be sure to use mat.

① Stand in upright position.
② Hold body stiff _ fall forward. Catch self on hands.

4. Hand stand.

① Hands above head. One foot raised.
② Swing arms and leg down _ other leg swings back and up followed quickly by other leg.
③ Balance _ arching back.

(NEED partner to assist.)

5. Double forward roll.

(1st: roll) (2nd. roll)

Cross ankles at end of first forward roll _ continue into second roll.

(See Forward roll. Grade 3.)

6. Forward roll over rolled mat or blanket.

① Two quick steps _ with spring extend arms over mat. TUCK HEAD. weight on arms.
② Roll over.   ③ Up on feet.

Figure 10-28

EVALUATION

For the Children

Each child in grades K-6 should be able to judge himself in stunts and tumbling according to his individual level of development, by answering the following questions to himself, in his own way:

Am I doing these activities in such a way that they help me to develop physical fitness? Are my muscular skills, my power, my coordination, and my balance developing? How could these activities help me more?

Socially, am I gaining in cooperation, courage, stick-to-it-tiveness, taking turns happily, and in good sportsmanship because of these activities? Am I a good captain when it is my turn to be one? Am I a good follower or member of my team? Do I really understand that people are different? Do I appreciate some of the good traits in others, even though they are different from my own? What should I do to help me more in this way?

Are stunts and tumbling so much fun for me that I like to do them at recesses or after school at home? Am I learning to control my emotions by doing these activities?

Am I learning how to think things through, step by step? Am I planning with other children, and helping them to carry out our plans? Do I know, understand, and use the safety rules? Do I help to make up other rules, and use them in case they are needed? Is my interest span getting any longer? Could I help myself more in this way?

For the Teacher

In the teacher's self-evaluation for the unit on stunts and tumbling, answering the following questions would be worthwhile:

Am I helping my class as much as possible to obtain their objectives?

Can I be enthusiastic about stunts and tumbling and get that enthusiasm across to the boys and girls?

Can I keep from assisting the captains too much—or from keeping order too much—except by my interest and presence?

Am I keeping watch, at all times, for each child's safety?

PART FOUR

Games and Sports

11

Learning by
Practicing and Playing

While games and sports may be classified in many different ways, they are grouped here under four types of activities. Chapter 12 includes basic game activities: lowly organized games, running-tag games, relays, and simple games using balls. This chapter is for grades K-3, though some of the games and many of the relays are also suitable for grades 4-6. Chapter 13 includes games for special occasions: holiday games, games suitable for the classroom, and outdoor winter activities. All children would enjoy these activities; they could also make up others that would be suitable. Chapter 14 consists of individual and dual activities for the primary grades with small group activities added for the intermediate grades; more detailed explanations of long rope jumping, marbles and hop scotch; and track and field activities, which can be done by children in all grades, adjusting the heights, distances and times for the different age groups or for the size of the children. Chapter 15 is on sports, with the emphasis on the skills involved, relays and lead-up games using these skills, and "six-man" games. Six sports are included: soccer, touch football, hockey (ice or field), basketball, volleyball and softball. This chapter is for grades 4-6.

In all of these games, speed comes with control, control comes with skill, and skill comes with understanding and practice.

OBJECTIVES

Games and sports help children learn how to act in a group; how to be good leaders and good followers. Children learn to take turns being "It." They learn how to help their captain and other children. They learn to see differences in other people and to understand them. They learn how to control themselves; how to play hard and yet have good manners; how to be a good sport, and what good sportsmanship really means. They learn how to play cleanly and fairly; how to have fun and help others have fun; and how to be honest—to admit their mistakes and take the penalty if there is one.

In order to get a lot of physical exercise in playing some games, children learn that they must have good body control and coordination. They must put their entire selves into their playing, stick to it as long as possible, and gain in both skill and endurance. They must educate their feet and legs as well as their hands and arms. They must use their heads at all times. Going "wild," or rough-housing, has no place in playing games. In order to have good games, can they help others gain in skill—and in thinking, too?

Do they know how to "play safe?" Do they know how to take good care of their equipment, and do they do it? Do they help make their playing area safer? How?

METHODS

Explain the game, and what the children need to know to play it. Keep all explanations short and clear. Practice the skills involved. What should they try to do to play well? Movement exploration can be used here to good advantage.

Divide the class into groups of six to eight. Be sure that all know their own boundaries. Steer the children away from choosing up just two teams. Somebody is bound to get his feelings hurt by being chosen last over and over. Sometimes go by the alphabet, using either first or last names; or go by birthdays. Keep all games short. Have the children play to win, but be sure that they all know that as long as they play as hard as they can, they have done well, win or lose. After a few minutes of very hard play, call everybody over and discuss any problems—or any good things—that came up. Guide them, but let the children do most of the talking.

Be sure that all know the safety rules: There should be no body contact in most games; all tagging should be without pushing in "It" games; keep the body under control at all times. Think. Help the children learn to settle their own problems as they play; and help them learn to umpire themselves. If somebody gets to showing off, call him over. Cool him off or rest him—then let him go back and play some more.

Some primary children are reluctant to try anything new. Let them watch. They'll probably join in the next day—or the next. Sometimes a child needs a friend or a buddy to play with him, to help him get started in each new activity. Sometimes he can do it on his own, as long as he understands what is expected of him.

Try not to eliminate children from a game. Instead, get a point called against them—or a foul—but stay in the game and try all the time.

Suggest that they play the games at recesses or at home. Have lots of fun and action. Play hard.

12

Basic Game Activities

Some of these games are for the entire group to do together; others might be taught that way, but are best played as movement exploration, in small groups, giving all more activity and more turns to be "It." Many of the basic body mechanics, skills and organization given under "Basic Ways to Develop a Physically Fit Body" need to be taught here, since many of the games give the children basic running, tagging and dodging practice as well as the basic groundwork for the chapter on "Sports."

These are all activities that the children like to do again and again. They are happy; they are learning; and they are having fun.

SECTION 1—LOWLY ORGANIZED GAMES

These games are to help the children learn how to play with each other, how to be a member of a group or team, how to take turns being "It" and how to play fairly so that all will have fun.

One method of teaching a game is to have one group of children demonstrate as the others listen and watch. Be sure that all understand what they are doing, why, and the safety rules. Then quickly get all groups started playing.

The games explain themselves very well. Enough are given here so that each teacher can pick the ones that best suit his purpose and his class. Remember that windy weather makes the children frisky and they need a lot of activity!

Follow the Leader

Best played in groups of four to six. All must do everything that the leader of the group does: such as, walk, run, hop, slide, skip, clap hands, wave, pretend to beat a drum, or anything else that the leader can think of. Take turns leading.

Huntsman

The "Hunter" says, "Who wants to go hunting with me?" The players in his group say, "I do." Then they say, "What are you going to hunt for?" The hunter names some animal, all make believe they're getting ready to go hunting, and follow him, quietly. He suddenly stops, aims, and yells "Fire"—as they all do the same. Then all rush back "Home." Whoever gets there first is the new hunter. If a player gets to be the hunter three times, change hunters.

Squirrel in Trees

Each two or three players make a "Squirrel house" by joining hands. A "Squirrel" lives in each house. One or two extra squirrels have no houses. On the signal, "Change houses," all squirrels change to a different house, including the ones with no houses. Only one squirrel may live in each house. The ones left out are "Slow pokes." Try never to be a slow poke! After a few minutes have different squirrels. Try not to touch anybody.

Simon Says

When the leader says, "Simon says," everyone must do as he does. If he *doesn't* say "Simon says," anyone who does it gets a point against him or must drop out. See who has the fewest points against him. Take turns being leader. Suggest that they use the physical education skills that they know.

Cat and Rat

The cat is on the outside of a circle of about eight players; the rat is on the inside. The cat tries to catch the rat. The circle tries to help the rat by only letting the cat get through once in awhile. They both go in and out of the circle. This is a very active game, since the circle keeps going up and down to either let the rat through or to keep the cat where the rat isn't.

Slap Jack

"It" walks around the outside of a circle of about eight players, stops behind somebody, taps him on the back, and says, "Slap Jack." Then he runs around the outside of the circle one way, and the one tagged goes the other way. Be sure to watch out and have no collisions! Whoever gets back to the empty space first is "It" next time.

Run for Your Supper

"It" runs around the outside of a circle, stops, and tags two players on their joined hands. He calls "Run for your supper." He stays there, and the two tagged run in opposite directions around the circle. Whoever gets back to the empty space first is "It" next time.

Puss in the Circle

Best played in groups of six to eight. A "Pussycat" squats down in the middle of a circle, which is his "house." The "Kittens" come as close to him as they dare, purring or meowing. Suddenly he jumps up and chases them back over a line, which is their "house." Any caught must stay in the "house." After three turns, see how many kittens are caught. Choose a new "Pussycat" and start over.

Back to Back

Stand on either side of a long line, back to back with a partner. On a signal, all start walking, hopping, etc. in the direction they are facing. When the leader claps his hands, all get back to their partner, join hands, and squat down, keeping their backs straight. Try never to be the last two down.

Tap the Bear

Best played in groups of six to eight. All players form a fairly large circle and stand with their hands behind their backs, palms open. The "Bear" has a "Bear's tail" in his hands—a knotted towel, an old piece of rope, or something else fairly soft. He puts it into somebody's hands, and then runs around the circle, being chased by the other one, who tries to tap him, with the "tail," not too hard, as many times as he can before the "Bear" gets back to the empty space. Tap only on the hips and legs.

Fire on the Mountain

Make a double circle, facing in, with a "Forest look-out" in the center. The inner circle of players are trees, who do not run; the outer circle are firemen, who run around the circle when the look-out calls "Fire on the mountain" and begins to clap his hands over his head. He suddenly stops clapping and runs in front of some "tree" and stays there. Immediately all the firemen get in front of "trees" too, one for each. Whoever gets left out is a slow poke. One of the faster ones becomes the new look-out. Now, the players who were first "trees" are the firemen, and the old firemen are the "trees."

Poison

Best played in groups of six to eight. A block of wood, or an Indian club, is stood up in the middle of the circle. All join hands. On a signal from their captain, all try to make the others knock the block down, by pushing and pulling. Anyone who knocks it down must drop out. If two players let go of hands they are both out. See who can stay in the longest.

Streets and Alleys

The entire class stands in three or four parallel lines, making the "Streets" by joining hands in their own lines. When the leader calls "Alleys," they turn a quarter turn right, and quickly join hands with the new people beside them, thus making alleys. When he calls "Streets," they turn back, and quickly join hands. One player is "It," chasing another one up and down the streets and alleys. They may not break through nor under joined hands, nor tag across them. If tagged, the one being chased becomes "It." Turn often. Once the players catch on, it is fun to play this game with two or three "Its," each one chasing another player. Watch out for collisions!

SECTION 2—RUNNING-TAG GAMES

In playing games, the children learn to see and understand differences in people. They learn that by playing hard and practicing they often can play a game better—and thus have more fun. They learn that they must have good manners and "Play safe" so that nobody gets hurt. There must be no tripping, pushing, or poking each other. They must keep their bodies under control.

Most of these games have been "turned around" from the usual way of playing them to the way that the children like best. This way, if a child is fast, he gets to be "It" longer, but not more than three times, so that others can have their turns at being "It" too.

As with the lowly-organized games, these games really explain themselves, and enough are given so that the teacher can have a good choice.

Tag

Tag is played either in two's or in groups of four to six, each group keeping within its own set boundaries. This helps the children try to dodge "It" rather than to just run away from him. If a player is tagged, he becomes "It." Does each group need a "Safety spot" where the children can take "Time out" if they need to?

Here are some ways of playing tag. Can the children think of others? Walking, running on tiptoe, skipping, sliding, "ankle" (played holding onto one ankle), "animal" (make the sound of some animal), "shadow" (step on somebody's shadow), stoop or squat (one is safe if he stoops or squats—he can only do this three times during a game.), "Chinese" (one must hold onto the part of him that was tagged), and Initial (write someone's initials on the board or ground—he must erase them before chasing the writer).

Space Men and Jet Pilots

The space men stand behind one line, while the jet pilots stand behind another line ten to fifteen yards away, with their backs turned toward the space men. The space men "creep up" toward the jet pilots as near as they dare—but not too close. Suddenly, the leader calls "Go get them, jet pilots!" Immediately the jet pilots chase the space men back to their own line. Any that get tagged must turn into a jet pilot. Now it is the space men's turn to chase the jet pilots.

Flowers and Wind

The "flowers" all choose to be some kind of a flower—they are all the same kind. During this time the "wind" is blowing loudly so that they can't hear what the flowers are saying. When ready, the flowers come as close as they dare to the wind. The wind says "Who are you?" The flowers say "Guess." When the wind guesses right, they chase the flowers home. Any caught must join the wind. Alternate being the wind and the flowers.

Animal Chase

Divide the group into three or four teams, each team choosing to be some kind of an animal. Each team lives in a different "field" or corner of the playing area. The "farmer" stands in the middle of the playing area and calls for one kind of animal to come out to run. He chases them, and tags as many as he can in half a minute. Any caught must go to the "barn" until all groups have been called out. Then all return and start over with a new farmer. See which farmer catches the most animals. See which animals never get caught.

Captain Midnight

This is best played in groups of about six. Captain Midnight stands with his back to the others, who are behind a line ten to fifteen yards away. They come as close to him as they dare and then ask "What time is it?" He answers by any time he wants. They keep asking until he says "Midnight!" Immediately he chases them back to their line. Any who are tagged help him to chase the others next time. After three turns, choose a new Captain Midnight, and send the others back to play again. See how many each Captain Midnight tags. See how many never get tagged.

Purple Tom

Same as Captain Midnight except that they ask "Who are You?" He answers by different colored Toms. When he says "Purple Tom," he chases them.

Hill Dill

This is best played in teams of about six. The players stand behind one goal line. The other goal line is fifteen to twenty yards away. "Hill Dill" stands in between and calls, "Hill Dill, come over the hill, or else I'll catch you standing still!" Immediately all players try to get to the other line without getting tagged by Hill

Dill. Anyone tagged helps Hill Dill next time. Play three times and then change to a new Hill Dill and start over.

Red and White

Have two teams, one "Red" and the other "White." The teams stand on either side of a center line, each one touching it with one foot. If the leader calls "Red," the whites chase the reds to a line about fifteen yards away. Any that get tagged must become a white, and may not be tagged back. When the leader calls "White," the reds chase the whites over their line. See which team has the most players at the end of the game. See which players never got tagged.

Bull in the Pen

Best played in teams of five or six. The "Bull" stands in the middle of a circle of players whose hands are tightly joined. He tries to break out. When he does so, the circle must count to ten out loud, and then chase him. Whoever tags him first becomes the new bull.

Snatch the Bacon

Best played in teams of five to eight. Have two lines of players, about ten yards apart, with the "Bacon" (a handkerchief, club, eraser or block) half way between them, on a spot. On a signal, the right-hand player from each line runs in and tries to get the bacon and take it back to his own line without getting tagged by the other one. If he does it, he gets a point for his team; if the other player tags him, the other one gets the point. Once a player touches the bacon he may be tagged. Take turns.

Gathering Sticks

There are many ways to play this game. Here is one. Have two equal teams, both scattered over their own half of the playing area, with a center line between and a "Prison" (about six by ten feet) near the back of their own area (see Figure 12-1). Have three *sticks*, blocks, clubs or erasers in each "prison" at the start of the game. The players are safe only on their own side of the center line. Each team should plan to have about one-third guards and two-thirds attackers. The object is for an "A" to get through to "B's" prison without being tagged by a "B" (or the other way around). Both attackers and defenders may tag an opponent who is on their land. If an "A" gets tagged on "B's" land, he must go to "B's" prison and stay there until he gets rescued by an "A" who gets through safely. If an "A" gets through to "B's" prison safely, and there are no prisoners there at the time, he may take one stick back to his own prison safely. If there is a prisoner or prisoners, he must rescue them, and *none* of them may take a stick back. They may go back to their own land safely as long as they keep one hand joined; if not, they may be tagged on the way back. He may rescue all the prisoners at once. A team wins if it gets all six sticks in its own prison at once. It may also win if it gets all of the other team in prison!

Capture the Flag is a similar game, each team having a flag on a pole in their prison. This game is usually played in a large field.

Prisoner's Base is another similar game. In this game, if an "A" gets through to "B's" prison safely, and there are no prisoners there, he wins the game for his team.

SECTION 3—RELAYS

Relays are enjoyed by children of all ages, as long as the teams are fairly short so that nobody has to wait too long for his turn. Five or six children per team is usually enough.

In doing relays, each child gets a chance to show how good a team member he can be, and usually a lot of team spirit is shown. Relays help the child learn to try hard and to stick to it, even though his team is way behind. This is a hard lesson for some children. Individual differences show up plainly in relays. Each child must learn that, as long as a child is trying as hard as he can, he is doing as well as he can, and maybe the others need to try

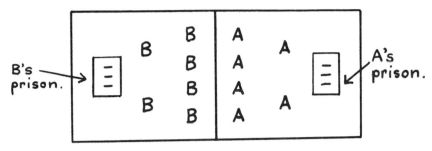

Figure 12-1

harder for the team to win instead of blaming a slower player if the team loses. Relays help each child to be a good sport in both winning and losing. The teacher can stress these points by discussing them with the children.

The team captain's job might include: trying to keep his team in position; seeing that all take their turns; seeing that each one gets close to the starting line but not over it until his hand is tagged by the one coming back; being sure that all understand what they are doing; and that all try hard. The captain is also the one to raise his hand when his team is finished. Be sure that all understand these points.

Once many of the basic body mechanics, skills and organization are introduced, they can be practiced in relay formation, as can many of the sports' skills.

Have fun! Try different formations for variety.

Formations (Figure 12-2)

1) Lines

A. The entire team goes at once, either over a finish line or around a block or marker, being sure to follow exactly the one in front of them. The team wins that first gets back to place, standing at attention, in a straight line.

B. The first one in each line goes up, either to a finish line or around a block or other marker, coming back to the starting line, and tagging off the next player on the hand. He then goes to the

Relays. (Relay Formations.)

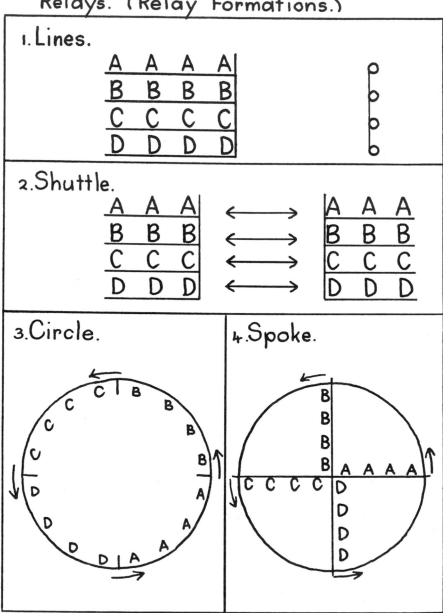

Figure 12-2

back of his line. The second player goes as soon as he is tagged. Continue until all have had a turn. When the last one gets back, he tags the captain's hand, who immediately raises it to show that his team is done. If the teams do not have the same number of players, somebody goes twice.

2) Shuttle Formation

Each team is divided in half. One half stands behind a leader, facing the other half, also behind a leader, ten to fifteen feet away. One player does the action (see "Ways of going)" across to the opposite leader, tags his hand, and then goes to the back of that line. The opposite leader goes across to the next one in the first line, tags his hand, and goes to the back of his line. Continue until all are back where they started.

3) Circle Formation

All teams stand beside their leaders in one big circle. The leader of each team does the action all around the circle, tags the next player, and goes back to place. Continue until all have been once. When the last one gets back to place, he raises his hand to show that his team is finished.

4) Spoke Formation

The teams each stand in a straight line, like the spokes of a wheel. The leader, on the outside edge of the spoke, does the action all around the outer circle made by the spokes, tags the player next to him, on his team, and goes to the inside, or hub, end of his spoke. Continue until all have gone. When the last one gets back, he tags the leader's hand, who raises it to show that his team is finished.

Ways of Going

Can the children think of others?

1) Ways of Moving:

A. Running on tip toes
B. Skipping
C. Sliding
D. On heels
E. Others.

2) Like Animals:

A. Chickens
B. Crabs
C. Horses trotting
D. Galloping
E. Elephants
F. Others.

3) Like Things that Go:

A. Airplanes
B. Jets
C. Boats
D. Trains
E. Automobiles
F. Others.

4) With a Partner:

A. Chariot Race—one hand must always be joined with partner's.
B. Back to Back—back to back with a partner, go sideways, keeping hands joined.
C. Coffee Grinder—run to finish line with partner, join both hands, hold them high, and go under them twice without letting go.
D. Wheelbarrow—one partner puts his hands on the floor with his feet apart, knees fairly straight; the other walks between his legs, and picks him up just above his knees, putting the wheelbarrow's knees on his hips. They move forward in this position. Be careful not to let the wheelbarrow down hard.

5) Using Something:

    A. Walking-on-paper (or block) relay—each leader has two pieces of paper. He stands on one, places the other one ahead, and moves onto it. Continue.

    B. Flag relay—carry a flag or a streamer. Be sure to keep it straight up for safety.

    C. Block, or eraser, or book-on-head relay—stand tall, but be careful. If it falls off, stop, put it on again, and continue.

    D. Kangaroo-jumping relay—hold a piece of paper, a ball, or an eraser between ankles. Hop.

6) All Up Relay:

Put two blocks, or erasers, in a square on the finish line. The first player runs up and moves them outside of the square, one at a time, one hand. He then goes back and tags off the next player who runs up and puts them back into the square, one at a time, one hand. Continue until all have had a turn.

7) "Potato" Shuttle Relay:

"Potatoes" are blocks of wood two by two by four inches. Erasers or bean bags could be used instead. Mark a square at the starting line and another one at the finish line for each team. Put two potatoes in the square on the finish line. The first player runs up, picks up one potato and takes it back to his starting line square. Then he goes back and gets the second one. When the second player gets tagged, he takes one back to the finish line square and comes back and gets the other one, making two trips in all. Continue.

8) Using Balls:

Besides using balls for relays for speed, these relays may also be done slowly for practicing skills in sports. See Chapter 15 on Sports.

SECTION 4—SIMPLE GAMES USING BALLS

These games give the children a chance to learn the basic rules for ball handling. Some will prefer to use bean bags at first in some of the games. The children must learn to keep their eyes on the ball at all times; to be ready to catch it or kick it when it comes to them; and to know what to do with it when they get it. They must never throw nor kick the ball to somebody who isn't looking. Have them call his name first to get his attention. Be sure that he is ready to receive it. Aim carefully. Be alert. When catching a ball keep fingers spread and pointing up if the ball is high; pointing down if the ball is low. Close the hands tightly on the ball.

Individual differences show up in this type of game too, since some children can throw and catch much better than others. Children learn to try to help others who cannot do as well, and to be patient with them. The slower child must also be a good sport, and keep trying. This will help him to be accepted by the others. (Be sure to discuss these points with the children. Have them demonstrate.)

Chase the Animal Around the Circle

This is best played in groups of six to eight, each group standing in a circle. Pass a ball, bean bag, or eraser from one player to the next. Watch it all the time. See if it can get around the circle without being dropped. Make believe it is some animal. Then start out another "animal" too, about half way around the circle from the first one. See if one animal can catch the other. As soon as a player passes one, he should watch out for the next one.

Hot Potato

There are two ways of playing this game, using either a ball or a bean bag. Be in groups of six to eight, each group standing in a circle. Way 1: On the signal "Go," each group starts to pass its hot potato quickly around the circle. Make believe it burns their fingers. When the leader calls "Hot potato," whoever was last touching it must drop out or get a point against him. Continue. Way 2: There is an "It" just outside of each circle. The players pass the ball around the circle in either direction, and "It" tries to touch it. When he does so he chooses somebody else to be "It."

Teacher Ball

This is best played in groups of four to six. All stand side by side, in their own group, facing "teacher" (another child) who has a bean bag or ball in his hand. He tosses it to the first player in line, who catches it and tosses it back. Continue down the line until all have had a turn. Then "teacher" tosses it to the first player again, who becomes the new teacher. The first teacher goes to the other end of the line. Continue. How else can children play this besides tossing it?

Keep Away

Two players try to keep a ball or bean bag away from a third player by throwing, bouncing, or rolling it quickly back and forth to each other, always keeping it within reach of the third child. If the third child touches it, one of the others is "It." This may also be played two against two.

Wandering Ball

Best played in groups of five or six. The players stand in a circle and pass a ball or bean bag one to another, in order, and in rhythm, as they chant: "The wandering ball goes round and round; to catch it safely you are bound; if you're the one to touch it last; why, then for you the game is past; and YOU ARE OUT!" The one touching the ball on the word "OUT" must drop out. See who can stay in the longest.

Circle Kick Ball

Best played in groups of six to eight, each group making a fairly large circle. Use an 8½" playground ball (or larger) for this game. See how many times the group can kick the ball back and forth and all around inside the circle before it goes out. Use feet and legs to stop it—not hands. If the ball goes out, begin counting over again. Keep the ball low, and do not kick it too hard. Be sure that all get many turns.

Club Guard

Best played in groups of six to eight. Form a fairly large circle around a player who is the guard of the block or Indian club. The club stands in a circle about four feet across, and the guard may not step in this circle. The players try to knock down the club by hitting it with the ball. The guard tries to keep the ball from hitting the club down, usually by keeping himself between the club and the ball. He tries to catch the ball and then throws it back to a different player. If the club goes down, or if the guard steps inside the club's circle, the last player to touch the ball is the new guard. This game may also be played by kicking the ball, keeping it very low.

Center Base

Best played in groups of six to eight, who form a circle around "It," who has a ball in the center. He throws it to any player in the circle, and immediately runs out of the circle. The player thrown to must put the ball in the center of the circle and then try to tag "It." In the meantime, "It" tries to tag the ball without getting tagged himself. If he succeeds, he is "It" again; if not, the other player is "It."

Dodge Ball

Best played, at first, in groups of about eight, who form a fairly large circle around one or two players. (Use an 8½" playground ball.) The outside players try to hit the ones in the center of the circle anywhere below the waist or from their elbows to their fingertips. The ones in the middle may go anywhere inside of the circle, trying to dodge the ball, usually keeping as far as possible from it. When a player gets hit, he quickly chooses somebody to take his place, and he takes theirs. Be sure that all get equal turns in the center. At first roll the ball; then throw it, keeping it low. As the players gain in skill they may have larger circles, and more in the center at once, up to half. In this way of playing, nobody goes in until all have been hit out; then all the others go in at once.

Boundary Ball

Have half the players on each side of a center line (see Figure 12-3). About six on a team is good. Divide each team in half; three are attackers, near the front, who try to make the points; the other three are defenders, or guards, who try to stop the ball from going over the end line behind them, and then throw it to their own attacking line. It counts a point every time a team throws the ball over the opposite team's end line. It is a foul to run more than one step with the ball; hold it more than three seconds; or knock it out of somebody's hands. If a foul is made, the other team gets the ball. Change attacking and defending lines about every two minutes. If this game is played outdoors, it is well to have one guard stand behind his own end line to get the ball quickly back into play. This game may also be played kicking the ball.

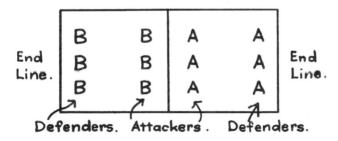

Figure 12-3

Bombardment

Bombardment is similar to "Boundary Ball." Add an end zone about three feet wide behind each team's end line. Stand six blocks or clubs in each end zone, evenly spaced. The object is to knock down all of the other team's blocks, by throwing the ball at them. Nobody may step into an end zone, and once a block is down, it stays down. Keep changing attackers and defenders.

Scrub Schlag Ball

"Scrub" means that everyone on a team of six to eight players takes turns at each position, each one playing for himself. When all have been "up to bat" once, that is an inning. Play as many innings as there is time for, though five or seven innings make a good game. If there are six on a team, there are three basemen, a pitcher, a catcher and a batter. If there are seven on a team, add a left short stop-fielder position. If there are eight, add a right short stop-fielder position. The order of rotation is third baseman to left short stop-fielder, to second baseman, to right short stop-fielder, to first baseman, to pitcher, to catcher, to batter, to third baseman. (See Figure 12-4.)

A five-inch rubber ball is good for this game, though a larger ball may be used. The "batter" throws a fair ball (that is anywhere in front of him, between first and third baselines or their continuation) and then runs to THE BASE (between first and second base) and back to home plate, tagging each with his foot. Whoever gets the ball throws it to catcher on home plate before the runner gets back there to put him out. The runner either makes his run or gets put out. Then all rotate, clockwise.

A caught fly is an out, so it is a good idea to throw a grounder. Players may neither hold the ball more than three

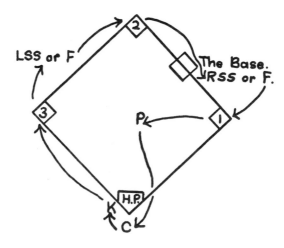

Figure 12-4

seconds, nor take more than one step with it. These are fouls, and the runner automatically makes his run.

This may also be played by kicking a soccerball, football, or playground ball; by batting a five-inch rubber ball; or by "fisting" a volleyball (hitting it with a clenched fist).

It may also be played one team against the other, everyone on the batting team coming up to bat each inning, while the fielding team rotates one position for each new batter.

Scrub Bat Ball

This is similar to Scrub Schlag Ball except that the fielding team tries to hit the runner with the ball, as in Dodgeball, before he can get back to home plate. This may also be played one team against another.

Scrub Kick Ball

There is no "THE BASE" as in Scrub Schlag Ball. The "kicker" runs to first base and back to home plate after kicking a fair ball. The pitcher rolls the ball getting it to go over home plate if he can. The kicker may either stand still and kick the ball or take two running steps as he kicks it. The fielding team gets the runner out by getting the ball to the first baseman on first base before the runner gets there; by catching a fly ball; by getting the ball to the catcher on home plate before the runner gets there; by tagging the runner with the ball in their hand; or by three strikes or four fouls (a miss is a strike). Rotate as before.

Kick Ball

Have two teams of six to eight players each, one team in the field and the other team up to kick. When the kicker kicks a fair ball (in the playing area, somewhere between first and third baselines or their extensions) he runs to first base, or further around the diamond to second, third, or home plate if he can. Once he stops on a base he stays there without taking a lead off the base until the next fairly kicked ball. A run is scored when the runner gets back to home plate safely. When everyone on a team has been up to kick once, no matter how many "Outs" there are, change places. An inning is over when everyone on both teams has been up to kick once. Five or seven innings make a good game. To give all a chance at each position, the fielding team should rotate positions either when every kicker comes up, when every two kickers come up, or at each inning.

Volleyball Newcomb

This is sometimes just called "Newcomb." Have half of the players on each side of a volleyball net, four or five feet high, depending on the size of the children. About six on a team is good, arranged as in Boundary Ball. The object is to throw a playground ball or volleyball back and forth over the net, keeping it within bounds (side and back lines) and trying to make the other team miss it. If a team misses the ball, throws it out of bounds, or makes a foul, the other team makes a point. Fouls are: taking more than one step holding the ball; holding it more than three seconds; or hitting it out of somebody's hands. The ball may be passed no more than three times before it goes over the net. The game may be played in five minute halves, ten minute halves, or until one team makes either fifteen or twenty-one points. It makes it fair for all children if both teams rotate every time either team makes a point. To rotate, each player moves clockwise to the next player's position.

Volleyball Twenty-One

Have a group of six to eight children in a circle, with the taller ones on the outside, acting as guards, and the smaller ones scattered in the center. Try to tap or push a beachball up above all players' heads twenty-one times without letting it touch the floor or go out of bounds. Use fingertip control, "giving" a little with the arms and wrists as one taps the ball. This could also be played in Boundary Ball position, rotating whenever the ball goes dead. With intermediate children it could also be played with a volleyball.

EVALUATION

For the Children

Am I learning how to play nicely with other children? Am I a good member of my group or team? Am I a good captain?

Will I happily take turns at being "It?" Will I play fairly so that all will have fun?

Do I understand why there are safety rules? Do I remember to follow them?

Am I beginning to understand that children are different? Do I still like them just the same? Will I gladly try to help somebody else? Sometimes do I offer to help without being asked?

Do I understand that I should be polite even in playing games? Can I still play hard and be polite all at once? Will I keep trying and stick to the game even though my team is way behind? Am I learning to be a good sport?

For the Teacher

Do I remember to teach basic body mechanics, skills and organization as they are needed for the activities for that day?

Do I use all of the possible space to good advantage for safety's sake?

Do I remember to stop a child after he has been "It" three times, both for his own sake and also to give others a turn at being "It?" Do I ask the children to help each other sometimes?

Do I help the children to understand that as long as a child is trying as hard as he can, he is doing as well as he can? Maybe they themselves need to try harder instead of blaming somebody else if their team is losing.

13

Games for Special Occasions

This chapter is divided into three parts: holiday games, games suitable for the classroom, and outdoor winter activities. With a little imagination, most games can be changed over to fit almost any holiday. By modifying the games just a little, many outdoor games and relays can be safely played in the classroom. Once the children catch onto how to change a game over to fit a holiday or their classroom, they can probably come up with many other ideas. In general, for outdoor winter activities, keep the groups small for greater safety and more action.

SECTION 1—HOLIDAY GAMES

Holiday games are very useful as the children are excited and here are constructive ways to use their energy. These games are also great for parties. Can the children change some of them to fit other holidays?

The following charts are very easy to read and understand, and should give the teacher many ideas. The left column gives the name of the game and the section where it is found from which the holiday games are adapted. Then the four principle holidays are listed with columns for possible games similar to the original. Of course there are many other possibilities. At the end, the Irish Jig for St. Patrick's Day, and the Maypole for any time during the month of May are listed.

Cardboard animals or such things (such as Figures 13-1, 13-2, and 13-3), six to twelve inches long, are good for some of the games: such as, black cats, turkeys, Christmas bells or trees and valentine hearts. The children could both design and color them. In many instances, adding the sound of the animal or thing makes the game even more fun to play.

Have fun! Be good sports! These are "extras!"

HOLIDAY GAMES

GAMES ADAPTED FROM _____

LOWLY ORGANIZED GAMES	*Hallowe'en*	*Thanksgiving*	*Christmas*	*Valentine's Day*
Squirrel in Trees	Owls in Trees	Turkeys in the Oven	Santa in the Chimney	Valentines in the Mailbox
Cat and Rat	Black Cat and Rat		Santa and Reindeer	
Run for Your Supper		Run for the Turkey		Run for Your Valentine
Puss in the Circle	Same			
Streets and Alleys		Ice Cream Chasing Apple Pie		Catch Your Valentine

Figure 13-1

RUNNING-TAG GAMES	*Hallowe'en*	*Thanksgiving*	*Christmas*	*Valentine's Day*
Tag in Groups	The Witch Catching Black Cats	A Farmer Catching His Turkeys	Santa Catching His Reindeer	A Child Catching His Valentines
Space Men and Jet Pilots	Ghosts and Witches			
Red and White	Bats and Jack o'Lanterns		Mistletoe and Holly	
Snatch the Bacon	Snatch the Jack o'Lantern	Snatch the Turkey	Cut Your Christmas Tree	Snatch the Valentine
	Captain Midnight			
	Purple Tom			
Hill Dill		Gobble, Gobble, Gobble		

RELAYS	*Hallowe'en*	*Thanksgiving*	*Christmas*	*Valentine's Day*

Have cardboard Jack o'Lanterns, cats, owls, witches, turkeys, nuts, fruit, Christmas trees, Christmas presents, bells, toys, reindeer, or valentines about six to twelve inches in size, and brightly colored or painted. In fact, the children can make them.

The following relays are especially good, though the teacher and the class can think of many others equally good.

Figure 13-2

In Lines, one at a time going			Deliver the Christmas Present	Mail the Valentine
In Shuttle, Circle, or Spoke Formation	Pass the Jack o'Lantern	Pass the Nuts		
"All Up" Relay	Owls or Black Cats	Fruit	Christmas Presents or Toys	Valentines

SIMPLE GAMES USING BALLS	*Hallowe'en*	*Thanksgiving*	*Christmas*	*Valentine's Day*
Chase the Animal Around the Circle	Owls, Witches, Cats	Turkeys	Bells, Deer	Valentines
Hot Potato	Hot Jack o'Lantern	Hot Potato or Hot Turkey	Pass the Christmas Bells	Pass the Valentines

Figure 13-3

Bombardment

Use only blocks to bombard, and have the proper cardboard pictures on top of them (see Figure 13-4). If the cardboard falls off the block it counts a point, and it stays off. A rubber ball is good for this.

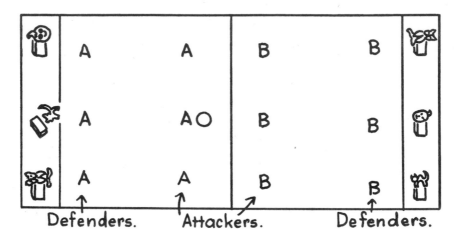

Figure 13-4

RHYTHMS	Hallowe'en	Thanksgiving	Christmas	Valentine's Day
Magic Carpet	Hallowe'en Magic Carpet	Thanksgiving Magic Carpet	Christmas Magic Carpet	Valentine's Magic Carpet
	Old Mother Witch	Ten Little Indians	Jingle Bells (Make up)	
		Sing a Song of Sixpence	Rudolph (Make up)	
		Indian Dances		

Chimes of Dunkirk—A turkey ran away, before Thanksgiving Day: He said, "They'll make a roast of me, if I should stay."

Shoemaker's Dance			Making Shoes for Christmas	
Broom Dance			Think up Presents for Christmas	

Here We Go Round the Mulberry Bush: Here we go round the Christmas tree. . . . What do you want dear Santa to bring? . . . . (The leader acts it out and the others guess what it is.)

GAMES SUITABLE FOR THE CLASSROOM	Hallowe'en	Thanksgiving	Christmas	Valentine's Day
Huckle, Buckle, Beanstalk			Huckle, Buckle, Christmas Bell	Huckle, Buckle, Valentine
Fruit Basket Upset		Thanksgiving Dinner Upset	Toy Basket Upset	
Pin the Tail on the Donkey	Put the Tail on the Cat		Put the Flame on the Candle	
			Put the Star on the Tree	

It is very appropriate to do the *"Irish Jig"* around St. Patrick's Day. The month of May is just right for doing the *Maypole.*

SECTION 2—GAMES
SUITABLE FOR THE CLASSROOM

At times it may be necessary to have physical education classes right in the classroom. Be sure that all of the children are aware of the need for safety. Have all breakable materials out of the way, and warn the children of any hazard that cannot be moved. Be sure that there is nothing on the floor or desks. Warn them to keep all hands and feet "in"—there must be no slapping, poking nor tripping others as they go by.

Have the children walk instead of run. Maybe a few at a time, or alternate rows play. Be sure that all understand why. Can they think of any other necessary safety rules? Here are some "safe" classroom games. They are also good party games.

Huckle, Buckle, Beanstalk

"It" hides some object in plain sight while the others keep their eyes closed. They all know what the object is. When "It" says "Ready," all get up and hunt for it, keeping their hands behind their backs, as they don't need to touch anything to find the object. When somebody finds it, he does not touch it, but instead, he quietly goes to his own seat, sits down, and says "Huckle, buckle, beanstalk." Keep on until all have found it.

Squirrel and Nut

"It" drops a "nut" into some player's outstretched hands, and then runs way around the room. He runs back to his seat, being chased by the other player. If he gets back safely, he is "It" again; if he gets tagged, he sits down and the other player is "It."

Cat and Mice

The "Cat" hides behind the teacher's desk. Four or five others are the "Mice." They tiptoe up to the desk and scratch on it. When the cat hears them, he jumps up and chases them anywhere around the room to see how many he can tag in a minute.

Pin the Tail on the Donkey

Stand a large cardboard donkey up on the chalk tray or easel; or stick a paper donkey up on the wall. Have a group of four or five children and enough "Donkey tails" so that there is one for each child. Have him put his name on it. Put a thumb tack or piece of sticky paper on the first child's donkey's tail. Blindfold him, turn him around once, and start him off toward the donkey. He must stick the tail on wherever his hand first touches the wall. Everyone has a turn. See who gets the tail closest to the right place.

Good Morning, Judge

"It" sits up front with his eyes closed and his back to the others. The leader points to somebody. That player disguises his voice and says "Good morning, Judge." "It" tries to guess who is speaking. He has three chances. If he guesses right, somebody else tries to fool him; if not, the other player is "It."

Changing Seats

For this game, the seats must be in rows, with aisles between, with the same number of seats in each row. On "Change right," all players move one seat to the right except those on the outside right row. They stand on the right side of their seats and quickly move around to the last row of seats on the opposite side of the room. They then sit down opposite the seat they were sitting in before. Other commands are "Change left," "Change front," and "Change back." If a player makes no mistakes he might possibly end up where he was at the beginning of the game!

Fruit Basket Upset

Each row of players is some kind of a fruit. Be sure that all know what they are. The leader calls two kinds of fruit, such as "Bananas" and "Apples." All "Bananas" and "Apples" stand up on the left side of their seats, and the row farthest left faces the back of the room. Then the leader says "Go." The "Bananas" and "Apples" must then exchange rows. The first row to be seated gets a point for their team. When the leader calls "Fruit basket upset," everyone must move to a different seat. In this case, each kind of fruit gets a point except the last kind seated. See which kind of fruit gets the most points—or which kind gets ten points first.

In and Out

One player chases another one around the room. The player being chased gets safe by sitting down beside somebody, thus causing that one to be chased. "It" may also sit down, thus causing the player he sits beside to be "It." Keep the game moving fast by sitting down quickly. Be sure that all have turns.

Numbers Change

All players have a number from one to six. "It" stands up front and calls two numbers, says "Go," and then counts to ten. The players having the two numbers called must exchange seats while "It" tries to tag them. If he tags one or both of them, he is still "It;" if not, he chooses a new "It."

Pick Up

Each child has a picture (or a piece of cardboard or scrap paper) on his desk. All stand up. On a signal from the teacher, all start marching, following a leader, winding up and down the aisles. They must be careful not to touch anything. When the leader calls "Pick up," all pick up the nearest picture in both hands and hold it up above their heads. The last one to do so is a slow poke. They set them down again and start over. Another way of playing is for the teacher to pick up three or four pictures after the class starts marching—or just before. When he calls "Pick up," the three or four without a picture are eliminated and must sit down at their own desks, keeping all parts of their bodies out of the aisles, for safety's sake. Continue in this manner.

Messenger Boy

Two teams are lined up in the outside aisle on opposite sides of the room, one team facing the front and the other team facing the back. Both leaders have a "Message" (a rolled piece of paper or an eraser) in their hand. At a signal, both leaders run around the room, outside of all the desks possible, back to their own teams, and give the message to the next one in line. That one immediately starts out, while the first player gets to the end of his own team without getting in the way of the runners. See which team finishes first.

Birds Fly

All stand. When the leader mentions anything that flies, all flap their "wings." When he mentions anything that does not really fly, he "flies" but anyone else that does so must sit down or get a point against him. See who stays up the longest, or who has the least number of points against him.

Scat

This is best played one row at a time. Be sure that all others keep their hands and feet out of the aisles. The players stand in line in front of the room, while "It" stands up back and leads them in an exercise. Suddenly he calls "Scat" and chases them all around the room, tagging as many as possible in one minute. Then a new group plays.

Numbers Run

The players in each row are numbered off from front to back. When the leader calls a number, all with that number *walk* up to the front of the room, back down their own aisles to the back of the room, and back to their own desk. The first one to touch his desk wins a point for his team.

Meet Me at the Switch

The room is divided into two teams, with each player having a number beginning with the outside front seat child as number one, the next one two, etc. Similar numbers should be opposite each other. The leader stands in front, center, with an eraser in each hand. He calls a number. The two with that number get up, come to him, get an eraser each, and continue walking around the room, coming back to him. Whichever one gives him the eraser first wins a point for his team.

And the Boiler Burst

One player walks slowly around the room, and up and down the aisles, telling a story. Suddenly he says "And the boiler burst!" This is the signal for all players to exchange seats. "It" tries to get a seat too. The one left out is a slow poke. "It" chooses a new "It" and the game begins again.

Home Run

Have the same number of players in each row. Number one has a ball, bean bag, or eraser. At a signal, he stands up, goes to the front of his row, and tosses or rolls the ball to number two, who also stood up. Number two rolls it back to number one and sits down. Then number three stands up, and number one rolls him the ball. Continue until all have had a turn. Then number one gives it to number two, who becomes "It" up front. Number one goes to the last seat in his own row, as all the others move up a seat. Continue until all have been "It," and number one gets the ball back at his own seat.

Schoolroom Snatch

Divide into two teams and get numbers as in "Meet Me at the Switch." Stand a block of wood up center front, with an eraser or cardboard picture on it. This game is similar to "Snatch the Bacon," except that the player tries to take the eraser to the back of the room instead of to his own line. Be sure that all children have their feet and hands out of the aisles.

Last Man

One player is "It" and another is the runner. The runner may keep himself from being tagged by stepping in front of some row and calling "Last man!" Immediately, the last one in that row is the one being chased, and all others move back one seat, with the first runner sitting down in the front seat. If "It" stops in front of some row and says "Last man," the back one in that row becomes "It." Move the game quickly.

Memory Run

Each row should be a team. The first player goes somewhere in the room, touches something, and calls it by name. He goes back and tags off the second player, who must touch and name the same object and then touch and name a second thing. The third player touches and names the first thing, then the second, and adds a third. See how high each team can go. If a player misses he must drop out, but the team continues. See which player can stay in the longest. All teams can play this game at once, as long as everybody is careful.

SECTION 3—OUTDOOR WINTER ACTIVITIES

All activities given here will probably not fit all schools, but some of them will fit the children and the playing area at some school, if the school is located where there is ice and snow at least part of the winter. Check with the school principal. Are these activities permitted in this school district? Is parental permission necessary?

Be sure that all children know, understand and obey the few safety rules that they may need to have. Have them stay far enough apart and get out of the way of others quickly. If there is a snowball throwing area, be sure that nobody wanders into it by mistake. Another safety hint is to have the children take short steps on ice or snow. This helps them to keep their balance.

Be sure that all children are dressed properly for the weather. In general, the activities should be done in small groups, for greater safety for all and to make sure that all are very active.

Sliding—flying saucers, toboggans, sleds

When the slider stops, he should get out of the way quickly and come back up away from the sliding tracks. Keep enough distance between sliders so that all are safe.

Skating

Allow no rough-housing on the skating rink. Try to avoid collisions.

Foot Slides

Each child should wait for the one ahead of him to get out of the way before he starts. Try to avoid "pile ups."

Skiing

Have the skiers in an area of their own, away from the sliders. Keep plenty of room between them so that all are safe. Have them come back up away from the skiing tracks.

Fox and Geese

This game is best played in new snow. Tramp out a circle about ten yards in diameter and make "spokes" in it, one for each "Goose." A group of six to eight is good for this game. One player is the "Fox." All the rest are "Geese." The geese are safe at the intersections of the spokes and the circle. The fox starts out at the hub. The geese interchange intersections by running around the circle and up and down the spokes, always sticking to the track. The track should be wide enough so that they can meet or pass each other. "It" must stick to the track, too, but tries to tag a goose. If he does so, the goose immediately becomes "It"—or the fox, and the first fox becomes a goose. Change quickly and move most of the time.

Snow Sculpture

When the snow is right, have groups of five to eight make whatever they wish. Sometimes a contest is fun. Discuss suggestions.

Snow Houses

One way of making a snow house is to put many snowballs a foot or two in diameter together, and build up on them. If there is a crust, cut pieces of crust and stack them together. Another way is to hollow out a house from a huge pile of snow.

Snow Forts

Snow forts are made by putting many snowballs a foot or two in diameter together and building up on them to the desired height. Stacked crust is also good if it is thick enough. Forts should be in the snowballing area, as this is what they are used for.

Snowballing

This should be allowed only in the area designated for it. Nobody should go there unless they wish to throw snowballs. Throw to hit rather than to hurt. The children might throw at snow forts; at snow sculpture in the snowballing area; or at certain tree trunks or other targets.

Snowball Throw for Distance

See who can throw a snowball the farthest—or over a certain line. Have one area especially for this.

Snowball Rolling Contest

See which group can roll the largest snowball in five minutes-or in ten minutes.

Other Winter Activities

Many physical fitness activities, stunts, games and rhythms that have a lot of activity may be played all winter outdoors, in good weather. Here are some of them:

Primary Grades (especially)

Follow the Leader	Fire on the Mountain
All kinds of tag	Space Men and Jet Pilots
Relays, all going	Hill Dill
at once	Physical Fitness Activities
Stunts	Keep Away
Rhythms	Tetherball

Intermediate Grades (especially)

Bull in the Pen	Club Guard
Red and White	Dodge Ball
Shuttle Relays	Ten Pass Keep Away
Stunts	Six-Man Soccer
Rhythms	Physical Fitness Activities
Tetherball	

EVALUATION

For the Children

Am I able to play holiday games without getting so excited that I forget to be a good sport? Can I keep myself under control while playing holiday games?

Do I understand why some things are safe outdoors and dangerous indoors? Can I play the indoor games quietly in a safe way and still have fun?

In doing outdoor winter activities, do I realize that taking short steps helps me to keep my balance on ice or snow? Do I help others keep in the right area for outdoor winter activities?

Am I a good sport about waiting for my turn in case I have to? Besides being a good player, am I a good watcher? Can I make myself really like to watch the others sometimes?

For the Teacher

Do I use the games for special occasions as teaching-learning situations? Am I as careful about teaching them as I am about teaching other physical education activities?

Do I plan carefully so that the children get as much activity as possible in classroom games?

Am I always "Safety conscious?" Do I help the children to play safely by going over the necessary safety rules or modifications with them, both indoors and out?

Can I get the children to see that they can have fun in playing these games without getting noisy? Do they understand that other classes in the school will like them better if they are quiet?

14

Individual and Dual Activities

Except for the three more detailed explanations of long rope jumping, marbles and hop scotch, this chapter is done with stick figure drawings, giving the teacher greater assurance that he is presenting the activities correctly. There is also a record chart for track and field events for the intermediate grades.

SECTION 1—INDIVIDUAL AND DUAL OR SMALL GROUP ACTIVITIES

If there is enough equipment, teach one activity at a time to the entire class. Then have them divide into groups of two or more, and continue as movement exploration. After a short time, call them together and introduce another activity. Be sure that all know and understand the necessary safety precautions (see Figures 14-1 to 14-5).

Another method is to divide into groups and have two or three from each group demonstrate what the teacher is explaining while all the others watch and listen. In this method, several activities could be explained. Then have all groups start, and after a short time rotate. Be sure that all groups have plenty of room and that all try very hard to keep full control of themselves so that there are no collisions. Keep thinking!

There is great carry-over value in these activities, as most of the equipment is simple and inexpensive. Many of the activities

Individual and Dual Activities_Primary Grades.

1. Toss and catch.

Toss   underhand.

Keep eye on ball.

2. Bean bag (or ball) toss and catch.

Ball must go just above head.

10 times right hand.
10 times left hand.
10 times right to left.
10 times left to right.

3. Bouncing balls.

Bounce catch.

Bouncey, bouncey!

Different rhythms.

4. Rubber ball kick for distance.

Running start.

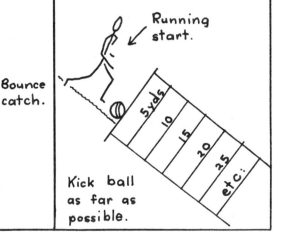

Kick ball as far as possible.

Figure 14-1

Individual and Dual Activities. Grades K-6.

1. **Balancing block on head.**

Keep good posture.

Suggested number of steps:-
Primary   50
Intermediate   100.

2. **Ring toss.**

Throw from 4-6 ft.

Intermediate grades take 4 shots from distance of 6 ft.

3. **Target throw into basket or circle.**

Use bean bags or balls.

Distance 5-10 ft.

(Throw underhand.)

4. **Target throw at block.**

Aim to knock down block. →

5 yards.

Intermediate grades take two shots.

(Throw ball underhand.)

Figure 14-2

Individual and Dual Activities_ Grades K-6.

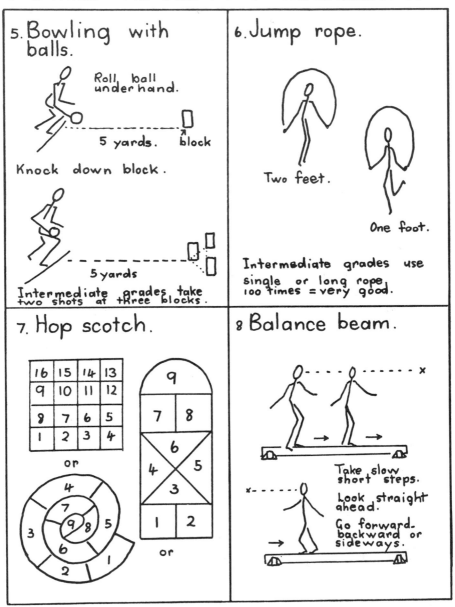

5. Bowling with balls.

Roll ball underhand.

5 yards.   block

Knock down block.

5 yards

Intermediate grades take two shots at three blocks.

6. Jump rope.

Two feet.

One foot.

Intermediate grades use single or long rope, 100 times = very good.

7. Hop scotch.

16	15	14	13
9	10	11	12
8	7	6	5
1	2	3	4

or

4
7
9 8 5
3
6
2 1

9

7   8

6

4   5

3

1   2

or

8 Balance beam.

Take slow short steps.

Look straight ahead.

Go forward, backward or sideways.

Figure 14-3

Individual and Dual Activities. Grades K-6.

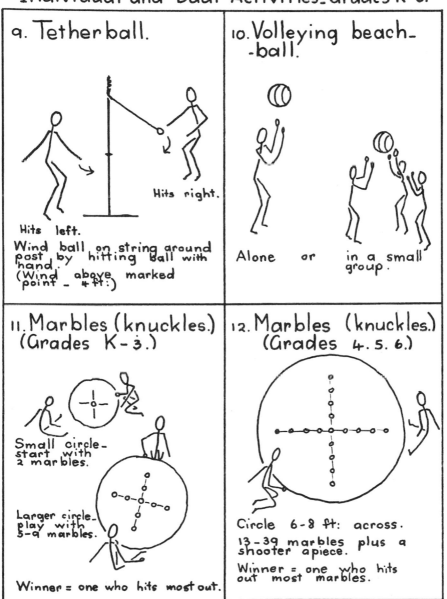

9. Tetherball.

Hits right.

Hits left.

Wind ball on string around post by hitting ball with hand. (Wind above marked point - 4 ft.)

10. Volleying beach--ball.

Alone   or   in a small group.

11. Marbles (knuckles.) (Grades K-3.)

Small circle-start with 2 marbles.

Larger circle-play with 5-9 marbles.

Winner = one who hits most out.

12. Marbles (knuckles.) (Grades 4. 5. 6.)

Circle 6-8 ft. across.

13-39 marbles plus a shooter apiece.

Winner = one who hits out most marbles.

Figure 14-4

Individual and Dual or Small Group Activities.
Intermediate Grades.

1. Deck tennis rings.

One hand catch.

When ring "dead"— both teams rotate clockwise.
Game 21 points.

2. Horseshoes.

Game 21 points.

To score- horseshoe should be on mat. or within 2 shoe widths of stake.

Nearest shoe = 1 point.
Leaner = 3 points.
Ringer = 5 points.

3. Featherball.

"Rotate" as in Deck tennis.

Play for 21 points.

4. Volleying.
(Beach or rubber ball)

Rotate clockwise.
Game 21 points.

Figure 14-5

can also be done alone, though it is often more fun to do them with somebody else or in a small group. Be a good sport. Help others gain in skill, too.

SECTION 2—ROPE JUMPING,
MARBLES AND HOP SCOTCH

The progression given here has proved to be good in teaching long rope jumping. If the whole class is doing this at once, have a long rope for every five or six children. Short rope instructions are pictured under "Individual and Dual Activities" (see Figure 14-3).

The following are Modified National Recreation Association rules for playing marbles, knuckling the shooter at the marbles trying to hit one or more out. A good way to start learning to knuckle is to have each child have a marble for a shooter, kneel down a couple of feet from the wall, and practice knuckling at the wall. His "shooter" is on his first and second fingers, in front of his thumb nail. The player makes the shooter go by snapping his thumb nail at it, quickly, aiming toward whatever marble he wants to hit. Once he can knuckle, he goes into the marble games given under "Individual and Dual Activities" in this chapter (see Figure 14-4), and then into the following modified official game.

The following rules are for playing one form of hop scotch, throwing the puck in, hopping and jumping in, and kicking the puck out. Hop scotch is sometimes played by picking up the puck instead of kicking it out. Three diagrams (Figure 14-3)for playing hop scotch are given under "Individual and Dual Activities" in this chapter.

Long Rope Jumping

A "long" rope is one that is ten to twelve feet long or more, swung by two children so that others may jump it. Use the whole arm in swinging the rope, and allow it to touch the ground each time it goes around once.

The following is a good order of progression:

1) Hold the rope still, a few inches off the ground. The jumpers line up.

   A. The first jumper stands facing the rope with feet together. He jumps over, both feet at once, landing lightly on the balls of his feet. He goes around one of the rope turners and back to the line of jumpers.

   B. The first jumper runs forward, leaps over the rope, taking off from one foot and landing on the other, and goes back to place.

2) Swing the rope back and forth, a few inches each way just off the ground.

   A. The first jumper stands near the center of the rope, facing one of the turners. As the rope comes toward him, he jumps it sideways, and continues around and back to place.

   B. Same thing, but continue jumping it as long as possible.

   C. Same thing, but run in.

3) Swing the rope way around, toward the line of jumpers.

   A. As the rope touches the ground, the first jumper runs in, under the rope before it comes around again, and out the other side.

   B. The jumper runs in and jumps the rope as it comes around as many times as he can.

4) Same as number three, but swing the rope away from the line of jumpers.

5) Try any of these ways, bouncing a ball on each jump.

Marbles

The ring (see Figure 14-6) should be ten feet in diameter, with anywhere from thirteen to thirty-nine marbles placed about three inches apart on cross lines, beginning with the center of the "hub." The marbles should all be the same size, not more than five-eighths of an inch in diameter, and not made of metal. The shooters should be made of anything except metal, and must be between half an inch and three-fourths of an inch in diameter.

From two to six players may play in a game, taking turns shooting.

The lag line is a line drawn tangent to the ring, and touching it at one point. A pitch line is drawn exactly opposite it. Before they start to play, the players lag to determine the order of

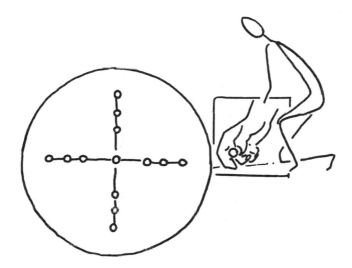

Figure 14-6

shooting. To lag, they knuckle down on the pitch line, shooting for the lag line. The player whose shooter comes nearest the lag line starts first, followed by the second nearest, and so on. For a second game, the winner of the first game shoots first, and the others lag for order.

The player shooting the greatest number of marbles out of the ring wins the game. A match may be one, three or five games. Marbles won are not for keeps. This is a game of skill.

To shoot, a player knuckles down at any point he wishes just outside the ring. At least one knuckle must be in contact with the ground until the shooter leaves his hand. If a player moves his hand forward, or raises it off the ground it is a foul, and he loses that turn. Any marbles that he hits out are his for the game, and he continues to shoot until he misses. Then, his turn is over, and he picks up his shooter. If he hits a marble out and his shooter stays in, his next shot is from where his shooter stopped; if his shooter goes out too, he shoots from anywhere on the edge of the ring. A marble stopping exactly on the ring is considered out. All marbles left in the ring stay where they stop, and the next player shoots at any he wishes to. A player must keep the same shooter that he lags with for the entire game. If he changes shooters he is disqualified.

If a shooter slips from a player's hand as he tries to knuckle, he calls "Slips," and may try again.

A player must not walk through the ring. If he does so he forfeits one marble, which is put back on one of the cross lines.

Hop Scotch

From two to six players may play in Hop Scotch (Figure 14-7), taking turns. The puck may be any size and of any material. Many people like a flat stone a couple of inches across.

The players lag for throws, by throwing their pucks at a line ten feet away. The one coming nearest plays first, and so on.

Start behind the baseline on one foot, holding the puck in one hand. Throw the puck into space number one. Hop in, and without touching any lines, kick the puck across the baseline. Then hop out. A player may hop as many times as he wants inside a space, as long as he doesn't touch a line. This would be a foul. It is also a foul if the puck stops on a line or lines, and if a player

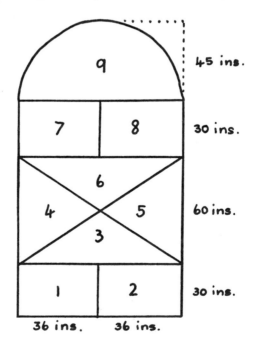

Figure 14-7

gets into or throws his puck into a space in the wrong order. The result is that he loses that turn. However, when it is next his turn, he begins where he left off before.

After a player makes space number one, he throws the puck into space number two. He hops into space number one; then into space number two; kicks the puck out and across the baseline; and hops out, first into space number one and then across the baseline.

He throws the puck into space number three; jumps into spaces number one and two, his left foot in one and his right foot in two, hops into space number three and kicks the puck out. To get out himself, he jumps back into spaces number one and two, one foot in each, and then hops out across the baseline. If the puck has reached only one of these spaces, he hops and kicks the puck out before crossing the baseline himself.

Continue jumping and hopping, when each is called for by the lines and spaces, until finishing space number nine.

Then, without the puck, the player makes one complete trip, both ways, jumping and hopping, until he hops out over the baseline.

Of course, if he misses or makes a foul his turn is over and he picks up his puck. Whoever finishes first, wins.

SECTION 3—TRACK AND FIELD EVENTS

The track and field activities are quite a challenge to intermediate children, who like to work on them in teams, with team captains, rotating activities after a short time. This too is movement exploration. The diagrams (14-8 to 14-12) explain the activities. Number 21 (pull-ups) is really for boys, though girls can try them too if they wish. Usually the girls do the flexible arm hang instead (see Modified Physical Fitness Tests in Part Two.) It would be well for a class to do one from each of the five types of activities one day; the second one another day; and carry on in this manner.

Primary children like to do these track and field events too, but be sure to keep the distances, heights, and number of times suitable for their age and size. For example, kindergarten children might race five yards, first graders ten yards, second graders

Track and Field Events. Grades 4.5 and 6.
Section A. For Speed and Endurance.

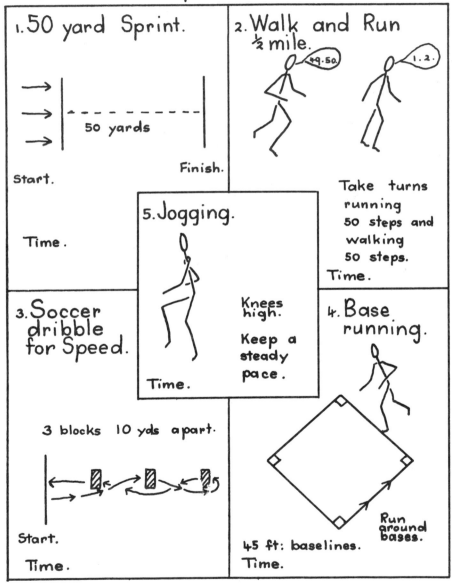

1.50 yard Sprint.

→

→   50 yards

→

Start.   Finish.

Time.

2. Walk and Run ½ mile.

Take turns running 50 steps and walking 50 steps.

Time.

5. Jogging.

Knees high.

Keep a steady pace.

Time.

3. Soccer dribble for Speed.

3 blocks 10 yds apart.

Start.

Time.

4. Base running.

45 ft: baselines.

Run around bases.

Time.

Figure 14-8

Section B. For Accuracy. (Aim.)

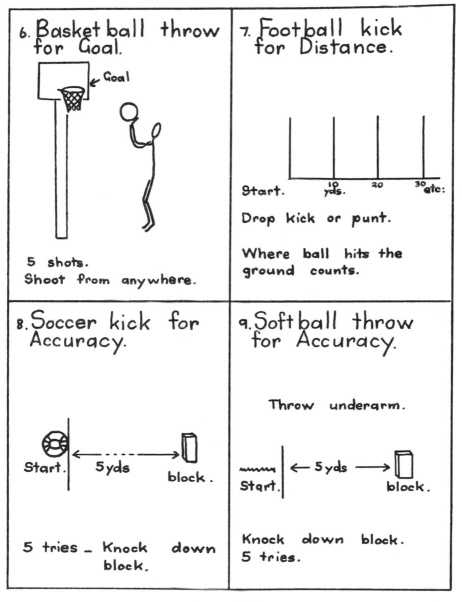

6. Basketball throw for Goal.

Goal

5 shots.
Shoot from anywhere.

7. Football kick for Distance.

Start.   10 yds.   20   30 etc:

Drop kick or punt.

Where ball hits the ground counts.

8. Soccer kick for Accuracy.

Start.   5yds   block.

5 tries _ Knock down block.

9. Softball throw for Accuracy.

Throw underarm.

Start.   ← 5yds →   block.

Knock down block.
5 tries.

Figure 14-9

Section C. For Arm Strength. (Distance throw.)

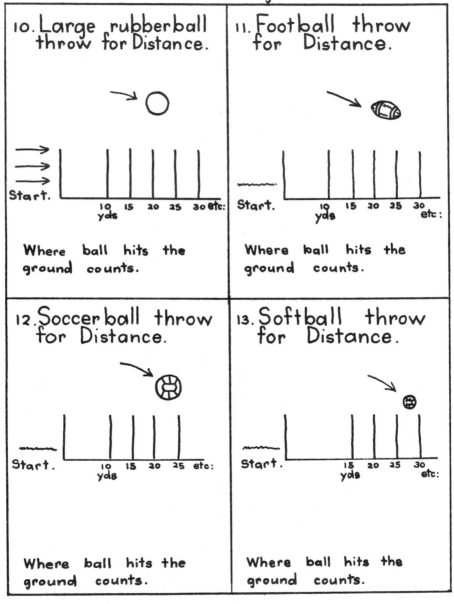

10. Large rubberball throw for Distance.

Start.

10 yds 15 20 25 30 etc:

Where ball hits the ground counts.

11. Football throw for Distance.

Start.

10 yds 15 20 25 30 etc:

Where ball hits the ground counts.

12. Soccerball throw for Distance.

Start.

10 yds 15 20 25 etc:

Where ball hits the ground counts.

13. Softball throw for Distance.

Start.

15 yds 20 25 30 etc:

Where ball hits the ground counts.

Figure 14-10

Section D. Jumping. Leg and Arm Co-ordination.

14. Running high Jump.

15. Running broad Jump.

Start.

Nearest part of body to start equals distance.

16. Standing broad Step.

Nearest part of body to start equals distance.

17. Standing broad Jump.

Nearest part of body to start equals distance.

Figure 14-11

Section E. For Arm, Leg and Abdominal strength.

18. Sit - Ups.

Hands behind neck.

Sit up - touch right elbow to left knee.
Lie down.
Repeat opposite elbow and knee.

Top Limit.   Boys 100.
             Girls 50.

19. Push - Ups.

Keep body straight.

20. Soccerball kick for distance.

Start.   10   20   30 etc:
             yds.

Where ball hits the ground counts.

21. Pull - Ups.

Girls do flexible arm hang.

Keep legs straight.
Do not touch ground in between.

Figure 14-12

twenty yards, and third graders thirty yards. The throwing and kicking activities might be measured in feet instead of yards. Another way to measure the throwing and kicking activities might be to name the various lines as *good, better, best,* and *moon shot!*

While the primary children are learning to do these activities, if enough equipment is available, the entire class might do first one activity and then another. With a large group, divide into three or four groups and for some of the events even have each child have a partner. Have lots of activity going on at once. When all understand, change to different teams doing different things, and rotate teams.

Use of the Record Chart for Track and Field Activities

In using the track and field activities record charts, have the intermediate children mark down the speed, the number of yards a ball is thrown or kicked, the number of baskets made or blocks knocked down, distances jumped, and number of sit-ups, push-ups, and pull-ups (number of seconds for girls for flexed arm hang) that they can do. Be sure that they mark down their results in the right columns for the season and their grade in school.

Each child should have two copies of the charts—one to take home after the unit is finished, and the other to go into his folder to be sent along to the next grade.

RECORD CHART FOR TRACK AND FIELD ACTIVITIES

PHYSICAL EDUCATION
STUDENT'S NAME   TEACHER: Gr. 4 _____
_____   Gr. 5 _____
SCHOOL _____   Gr. 6 _____

	GRADE 4		GRADE 5		GRADE 6	
EVENTS	Fall	Spring	Fall	Spring	Fall	Spring
For Speed and Endurance						
1) 50 yd. sprint						
2) Walk and run ½ mile						
3) Soccer dribble for speed						

EVENTS	Fall	Spring	Fall	Spring	Fall	Spring
4) Base running						
5) Jogging						
For Accuracy (Aim)						
6) Basketball throw for goal						
7) Football kick for distance						
8) Soccer kick for accuracy						
9) Softball throw for accuracy						
For Arm Strength (Distance Throw)						
10) Large rubberball throw for distance						
11) Football throw for distance						
12) Soccerball throw for distance						
13) Softball throw for distance						
Jumping—Leg and Arm Coordination						
14) Running high jump						
15) Running broad jump						
16) Running broad step						
17) Standing broad jump						
For arm, Leg, and Abdominal Strength						
18) Sit-ups						
19) Push-ups						
20) Soccerball kick for distance						
21) Pull-ups (Chin-ups) (Flex. arm hang for girls) (See Phy. Fit. Tests)						

EVALUATION

For the Children

Do I understand the rules enough so that I can carry on these activities at home?

Can I think of what I am doing now—not of what I am going to be doing next?

Am I willing to practice these events? If so, do I improve my playing—am I getting better results?

Do I understand how to use the record charts for the track and field events? Will I be fair in marking myself? Will I actually put down exactly what my best result is?

For the Teacher

Have I given all groups plenty of room? Have I reminded the children to think of what they are doing now—not of what they will be doing next?

Have I asked the children to try to keep full control of themselves—to have no collisions, to bother nobody else?

Have I told the children that these are good activities to carry on by themselves or with somebody else at home?

Have I explained how to use the record charts for track and field events? Am I sure that all understand? Have I suggested that they practice a lot?

15

Sports

The six team sports of soccer, touch football, hockey (field or ice), basketball, volleyball and softball are given for the intermediate grades. With the exception of touch football, these games may be played by both girls and boys.

In each sport, the emphasis is on the skills involved. These fundamental skills are given with stick figures and short explanations. The fundamental skills are followed by relays, involving practicing these skills. The relays should be done slowly at first to learn the skills, and then speeded up to see which team wins. Many of the relays given under one sport could also be used for others. Be sure to refer to the page of stick figures of the fundamental skills for the proper techniques.

The relays are followed by lead-up games, also involving practicing the skills. Besides being lead-up games, they are also games in themselves. Start the games with each group in a fairly small area, and gradually increase the area as skill develops. This is a form of movement exploration.

The six-man games, or modified team games, come after the lead-up games. In softball this could be a modified nine-man game. However, usually the six-man games keep the teams smaller so that all can be active but under their captain's control at all times, and so that they can all learn teamwork easier.

For safety's sake, in playing hockey, polyethylene hockey sticks, balls and pucks are very good, and can be used both indoors and out.

Soccer

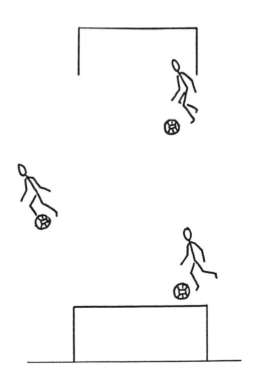

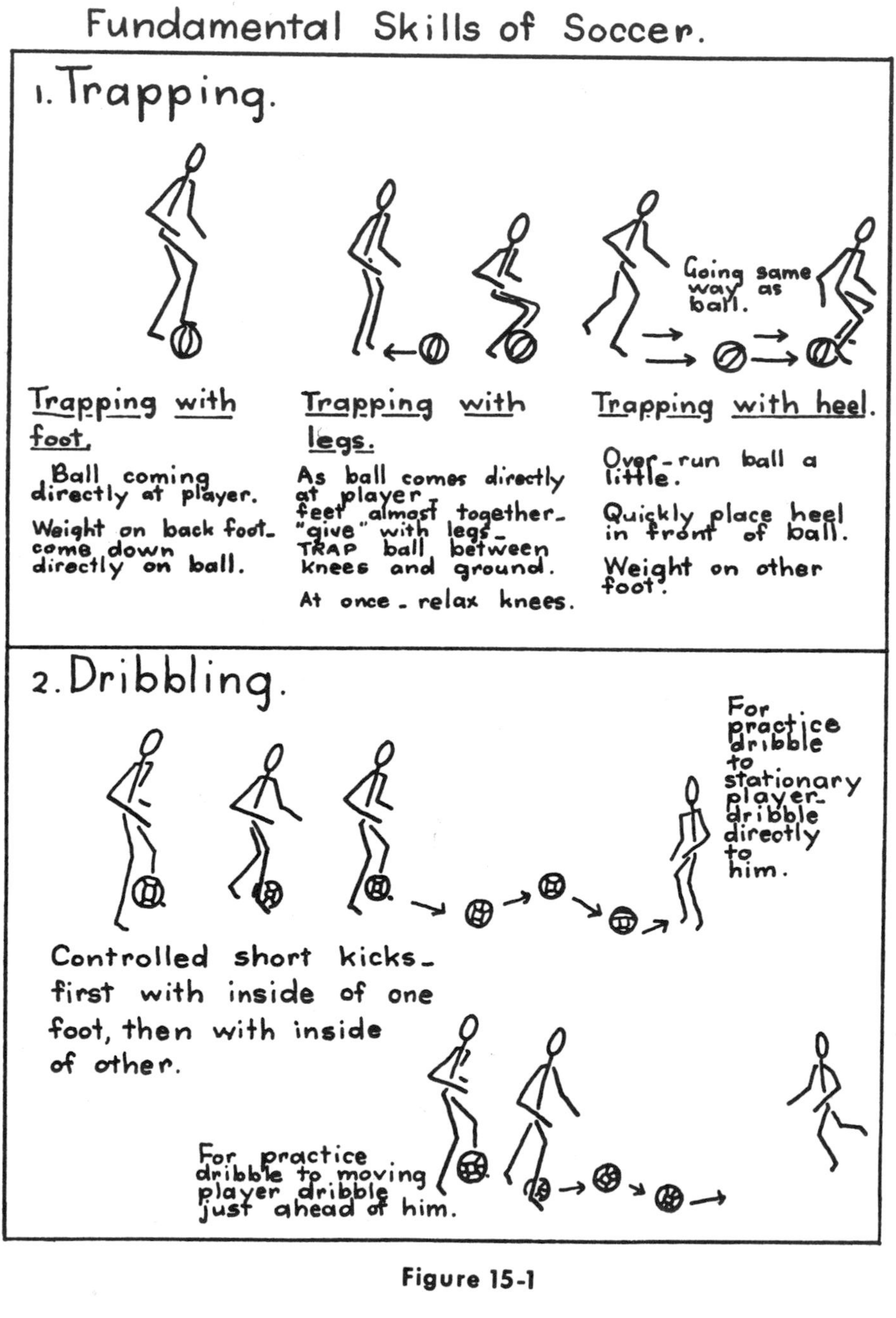

Fundamental Skills of Soccer.

1. Trapping.

Trapping with foot.

Ball coming directly at player.

Weight on back foot. come down directly on ball.

Trapping with legs.

As ball comes directly at player. feet almost together. "give" with legs. TRAP ball between knees and ground.

At once. relax knees.

Trapping with heel.

Going same way as ball.

Over-run ball a little.

Quickly place heel in front of ball.

Weight on other foot.

2. Dribbling.

Controlled short kicks. first with inside of one foot, then with inside of other.

For practice dribble to stationary player. dribble directly to him.

For practice dribble to moving player dribble just ahead of him.

Figure 15-1

Fundamental Skills of Soccer.

3. Kicking.

Kick stationary ball with instep or side of foot. Either standing or running start.

With rolling ball - time speed of ball, and kick as for stationary ball.

4. Passing.

to pass to a stationary player, pass directly to the player with inside of foot.

to pass to a moving player - pass slightly ahead of player, using inside of foot.

5. Running and dodging.

Trap ball, leg or foot and pass.

Trap ball leg or foot and dribble.

Trap - heel - side step - leaving ball for team mate.

Feint pass (fake) - make believe to pass, but keep ball.

Still has it!

Figure 15-2

SOCCER RELAYS

Soccer Kick and Trap

Shuttle formation-use all three traps.

Soccer Dribble and Trap

Shuttle formation (Figure 15-3).

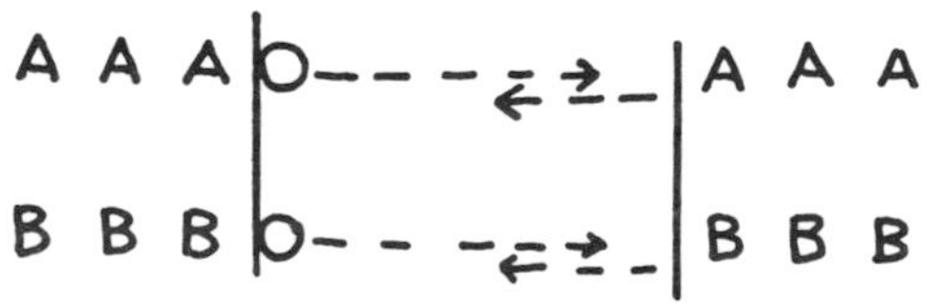

A A A O– – – ⇄ ⇒ – A A A

B B B O– – – ⇄ ⇒ – B B B

Figure 15-3

Soccer Dribble the Ball

Line formation—dribble the ball between two blocks about ten feet apart, around the second block, and back between the two blocks (figure eight.)

Soccer Dribble the Ball and Kick

Line formation—dribble the ball between two blocks, around the second block, and kick it back to the next one in line (see Figure 15-4).

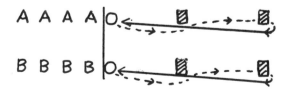

Figure 15-4

Soccer Dribble

Circle formation
Spoke formation

Soccer Kick for Distance (Figure 15-5)

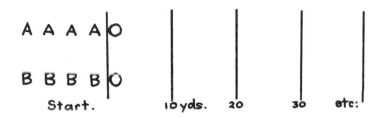

Figure 15-5

Soccer Dribble and Kick to Each Other

Double shuttle formation—two lines of players about three yards apart facing two other lines of players who are behind a goal about four yards wide. The two leaders go at once, dribbling and kicking the ball to each other until one kicks it through the goal.

Soccer Dribble and Kick to Each Other,
Dodging Two Stationary Players

Double shuttle formation—the two leaders go at once, dribbling and kicking the ball to each other, dodging the two leaders from the opposite lines, who have come about two yards ahead of their goal, and stand there until the others get by them.

Soccer Dribble and Kick to Each Other,
Dodging Two Movable Players

Double shuttle formation—same as above, but the two opposite leaders try to break up the passes, get control of the ball, and, running and dodging, dribble and kick it to where it started (see Figure 15-6).

Figure 15-6

Two Players Dribble and Kick for Goal, Guarded by one Player

Two lines of players about three yards apart facing the goal; have one line of players behind the goal—the leader of this line moves up about two yards in front of the goal, to act as the "Goalie"; the other two dribble and kick the ball to each other, and try to make a goal. The goalie tries to stop them. Rotate.

Three or Four Players Dribble and Kick for Goal, Guarded by Two Players

Have three or four lines of players facing the goal, with two lines of players behind it (see Figure 15-7). The leaders of the two lines move up in front of the goal and try to defend it; the other three or four attack it. Rotate.

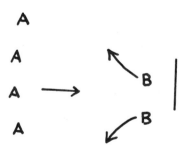

Figure 15-7

SOCCER LEAD-UP GAMES

Soccer Teacher Ball

Played kicking and trapping the ball (Figure 15-8).

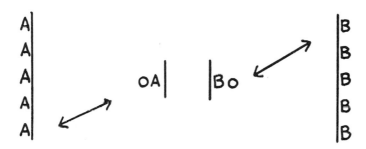

Figure 15-8

Soccer Dodge Ball

Played kicking and trapping the ball. Keep the ball low by turning the toes in toward it just as it leaves the foot. A player mustn't use his hands except to save his face in case the ball goes up in the air (see Figure 15-9).

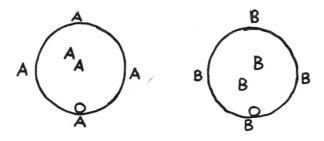

Figure 15-9

Soccer Club Guard

Played kicking and trapping the ball (Figure 15-10). Keep the ball low. No hands except to save the face.

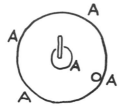 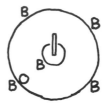

Figure 15-10

Ten Kick Keep-Away

There are two teams, attackers and defenders or guards, made up of three or four players each. Spread out, each guard guarding an attacker. The attackers try to kick or dribble the ball back and forth to each other ten times while the guards try to get control of the ball. Count each pass to another player on the same team as one. If the guards get the ball, the attacking team's score is erased, they become guards and the old guards become attackers and try to make ten kicks. Any bodily contact is a foul, and the teams change positions. Move the game quickly. Get away from each other.

Square Soccer, Circle Soccer or Line Soccer

Arrange two teams so that each team forms two adjacent sides of a square, half of a large circle, or one line facing the other team. Each player has a number from one to three or four, depending upon the size of the class. The teacher calls a number and rolls the ball toward the center of the playing area. All children having the number called run in and try to kick the ball over the line behind the other team, below their knees. All the other players try to block the ball and trap it, so that their team members in the center can get it. There must be no bodily contact, and hands are used only to save the face. It counts one point each time the ball goes out. Then, those players go back, and another number is called.

Circle Pin Soccer

Arrange teams and number as in Circle Soccer (Figure 15-11). Stand up two blocks (or Indian clubs or pins) four yards apart for the goal opposite the center of each team, and about two yards in from the outside edge of the circle. The object is to make a goal by kicking or dribbling the ball over the opponent's goal line, between the two blocks. Players having the number called may go all over the playing area, but it is well to have some stay back in front of their goal to act as defenders while others are the attackers. Play ten minute halves, or until a certain score is reached, as ten, fifteen, or twenty-one.

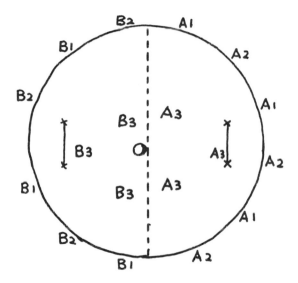

Figure 15-11

Six-Man Soccer

Have two teams of six players each, three attackers and three defenders, arranged on their own half of a rectangular court. Have a goal in the center of each end line, four yards wide marked by a block or post at each end. Place the ball at the center of the center line, in front of one team's center attacker. He then kicks off, probably to one of his "insides." All six attackers may go the full length of the field, trying to keep more or less in line with the ball, and trying to kick it to their own team-mates before their opponents can get it. The two side attackers should stay on their own side of the center attacker. All defenders must stay on their own side of the center line, and they try to have two of them between the ball and their goal. One defender is the goalie and stays quite close to the goal. Defenders try to kick the ball just ahead to one of their own attackers so that they can dribble or kick it down the field. If a goal is made, both teams change attackers and defenders, also changing side to center positions. The opposite team now kicks off. If no goal is made after about three minutes, change positions. Try to get a lot of teamwork in this game. Keep control of the ball. Try to get into a good position to receive the ball—both attack and defend well. Run fast—be a quick thinker. Play to win, have fun, play fairly.

Touch Football

Fundamental Skills of Touch Football.

1. Throwing and catching.

Hold fingers over laces.

Catch ball - pull in to body. tuck ball close into side. (Hold tip in hand.)

To "spiral" ball let ball roll off 4th and little fingers, as throw it.

As weight changes to other foot throw.

Catching. Face ball, catch both hands, with fingers spread and thumbs up.

Run!

Throwing. Weight on back foot - Right shoulder back. Tip of ball by ear.

At once pull ball in.

2. Kicking.

Holder on one knee.

Drop kick. Ball held up and down - waist high. One hand each side.

Keep eye on ball.

Punt. Hold ball - right hand in back, left hand on side.

Kick off. Ball angled to kicker. Held 1st finger, arms length away. Kicker kicks ball at base, with toe.

Ball tipped slightly away from kicker - shoulder high.

Weight on left foot.

Just as ball leaves hands kick it with instep.

Drop ball and kick with toe just as it bounces off ground.

Figure 15-12

Fundamental Skills of Touch Football.

3. Blocking : Tagging.

Blocking.
Keep self between opponent and ball carrier.

If carrier is touched two hands. he is **Tagged.**

4. Centering.

Feet apart. Both knees bent.
Eyes on ball.
Both hands on ball. Ball on ground.

On signal pass ball to receiver between legs.

5. Running and dodging.

sidestep.

Carrier zigzags when necessary by sidestepping, ducking etc. to avoid being tagged.

duck.

Figure 15-13

FOOTBALL RELAYS

Football Pass and Catch

Shuttle formation

Punt or Drop Kick and Catch

Shuttle formation

Center and Pass to Running Player (Figure 15-14)

Figure 15-14

Center and Pass, Punt and Receive (Figure 15-15)

Figure 15-15

Football Kick for Distance (Figure 15-16)

Kick off
Punt
Drop kick

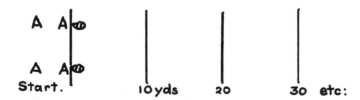

Figure 15-16

Blocking and Tagging, Two by Two

Double shuttle—two hand tag

Zig Zag Running and Dodging (Figure 15-17)

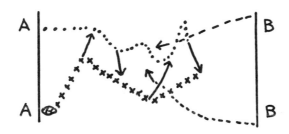

Figure 15-17

TOUCH FOOTBALL LEAD-UP GAMES

Center Base

Played with a football, to practice passing, running and dodging (Figure 15-18).

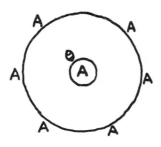

Figure 15-18

Club Guard

Played with a football to practice throwing and catching (see Figure 15-19).

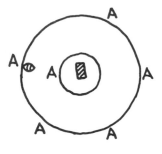

Figure 15-19

Kick Ball

Played with a football, the kicker receives the ball from the pitcher. The kicker may then kick off, drop kick or punt the ball. Otherwise, play the game like Kick Ball.

Beat the Ball

Similar to Kick Ball. After the kicker kicks off at home plate, he must run all the bases in order until he gets back to home plate. Whoever gets the ball must throw it to the first baseman, who throws it to second, who throws it to third, who throws it to the catcher at home plate. If the runner gets to home plate first, he is safe and makes a run; if the ball gets there first, he is out.

Ten Pass Keep-Away

Similar to Soccer Ten Pass Keep-Away, but played passing a football (see Figure 15-20).

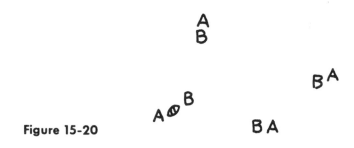

Figure 15-20

Punt Back

Have two teams of six players each, each on its own half of the playing area. One player has a football; that team lines up about half way down its own half of the field. The player with the ball punts it as far as he can toward his opponent's goal line. The opponents try to catch the ball on the fly, or recover it as soon as possible. Then they punt from the spot where they recovered the ball. The game continues, each side punting in turn, and each player on each team taking his turn at punting, no matter who recovers the ball. Each team is trying to move forward, toward its opponent's goal, until the players get close enough so that they can punt the ball so that it hits the ground, or is caught behind the opponent's goal line, thus winning a point for their team. Then the other team starts the ball. Change goals midway through the game.

Two-Hand Touch Football, Modified, or Six-Man Two-Hand Touch

Have two teams of six players each, lined up with three in front and three behind. Except for the two-hand touch, there should be no body contact in this game. Start the game with a kick off from the forty yard line. The receiver may advance the ball by a running play or a forward or lateral pass. Upon being touched two hands by the kicking team, the ball is dead, but the receiving team keeps possession of it and puts it in play by a scrimmage. In order to keep possession of the ball, they must advance it ten yards from the line of scrimmage in four downs. In case a forward pass is incomplete, the down counts, and the next play starts at the spot of the preceeding down. If a team wants to kick from scrimmage, it must call "Punt formation" and must punt, or give up the ball. If a defensive player intercepts a pass or catches a punt, he tries to return the ball across his opponent's goal line. If tagged two hands, the ball is placed for a first down at the point where he was tagged, and his team now has four downs to go ten yards. If a team carries the ball across the opponent's goal line, completes a forward pass in their end zone, or recovers a fumble in their end zone, it is a touchdown, and counts six points. Then, the ball is put in play as at the start of the game, the team scored upon having their choice of kicking or receiving. If the ball becomes dead in possession of a team behind its own goal line—if the defending team sent it across, it is a safety and scores two points for the other team; then the team scored upon puts the ball in play by a kick off; if the attacking team sent it across, it is a touchback, and scores no points; the defending team puts it in play on the nearest zone line. If a player crosses the line of scrimmage before the ball is snapped, he is offside and the penalty is five yards. Other fouls are: trying to interfere with a player trying to catch a forward pass; blocking a player; holding, tripping, pushing or any other unsportsmanlike act; the penalty is fifteen yards from the preceeding down for interfering with a player trying to catch a forward pass, and from the spot where the foul was made for the others. The game is usually played in quarters of six or eight minutes.

Hockey—
Field (with Ball),
Ice Hockey (with Puck)

Fundamental Skills of Hockey_
Field (with ball) and/or Ice (with puck.)

1. Stopping ball.

With foot_ raise
toes off ground
and bring down.
on to ball.
Do not kick.

With stick _ "give" a little
as stop ball.
Keep stick near ball ready
to hit.

2. Passing.

Keep stick
low_ hand
part
way
down handle.

Aim just ahead of receiver.

To complete stroke
turn toe of stick
down to avoid
"sticks" foul.

3. Dribbling.

Keep ball close to
stick _ right hand
part way down
handle.

Give ball many
short hits.

Control ball by
turning toe of
stick in and out.

Figure 15-21

Fundamental Skills of Hockey_
Field (with ball) and/or Ice. (with puck.)

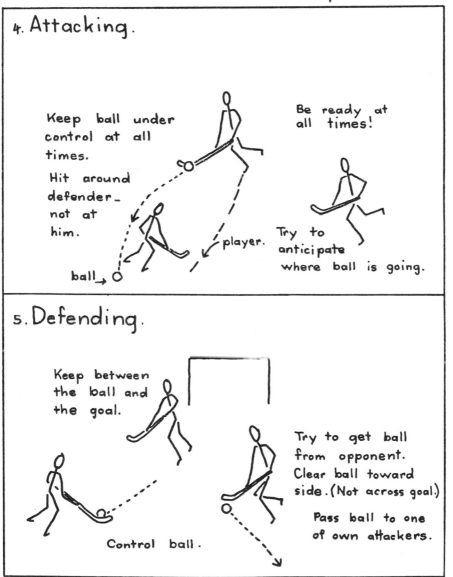

4. Attacking.

Keep ball under control at all times.

Hit around defender_ not at him.

Be ready at all times!

Try to anticipate where ball is going.

player.

ball→ O

5. Defending.

Keep between the ball and the goal.

Try to get ball from opponent. Clear ball toward side. (Not across goal.)

Pass ball to one of own attackers.

Control ball.

Figure 15-22

HOCKEY RELAYS

Hit and Stop (use either ball or puck)

> Shuttle formation:
>> Stop with foot
>> Stop with stick

Dribble and Stop

> Shuttle formation:
>> Stop with foot
>> Stop with stick

Dribble Figure Eight

Line formation—dribble ball or puck between two blocks about ten feet apart, around the second block, and back between the two blocks (see Figure 15-23). Keep control.

Figure 15-23

Dribble

> Circle formation
> Spoke formation

Two Versus One Hit for Goal

Two players dribble and hit the ball or puck back and forth to each other as they advance on the goal, which is guarded by one player (Figure 15-24). The two players try to make a goal.

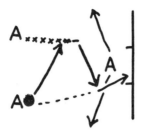

Figure 15-24

Three or Four Versus Two Hit for Goal

Three or four players dribble and hit the ball or puck back and forth to each other as they advance on the goal, which is guarded by two players. The three or four players try to make a goal (Figure 15-25).

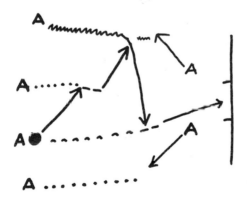

Figure 15-25

HOCKEY LEAD-UP GAMES

Hockey Teacher Ball

Played hitting and stopping the ball (Figure 15-26).

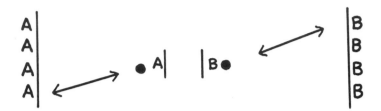

Figure 15-26

Snatch the Hockey Ball

Similar to Snatch the Bacon, but played hitting and dribbling the hockey ball or puck back to place (Figure 15-27).

Figure 15-27

Hockey Club Guard

Played hitting the hockey ball or puck. Keep the ball or puck low, and the sticks low, too (Figure 15-28).

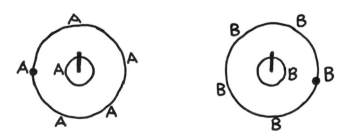

Figure 15-28

Ten Hit Keep-Away

Similar to Soccer Ten Kick Keep-Away, but played hitting the ball or puck (see Figure 15-29).

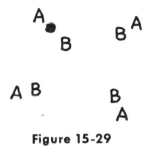

Figure 15-29

Six-Man Hockey

Similar to Six-Man Soccer, but played hitting a hockey ball or puck (Figure 15-30).

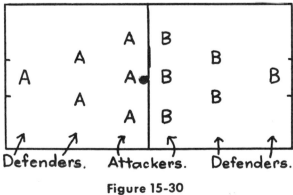

Figure 15-30

Basketball

Fundamental Skills of Basketball.

1. Passing and Catching.

Chest Pass.

① Feet apart.
Finger tip control.
Elbows in.
Ball chest high.

② Straighten arms as throw.

Weight front foot.

Fingers apart.
"Give" as catch.

Underarm Pass.

① Pull back a little.

② Pass low.

Bounce Pass.

Hold ball both hands. waist high.

Ball hits ground 3 ft. from receiver.

Catch about waist high.

Ball held close to body between waist and knees.

Overhead Pass.

A passes to B over head of guard.

Guard.

2. Guarding.

Guard. Stay between opponent and goal.

Move with him.

Be alert.

High.

low.

Keep eyes on ball.

Be ready to move in any direction.

Figure 15-31

Fundamental Skills of Basketball.

3. Goal Shooting.

Chest Shot.

① Relaxed all way through. Ball chest high.

② Slight downward-inward rotation of ball.

③ Straighten body as ball is shot. Aim just above rim.

Lay up shot.

Very close to goal.

As jump up right knee goes up – right arm up.

Bank shot on back board.

4. Pivoting.

One foot stays in same spot.

Knees bent.

Other foot moves in all directions.

5. Dribbling.

Head up.

Hands and ball low.

Weight on balls of feet.

Watch where going. Keep control.

6. Running and Dodging.

Ways to dodge.

Pass quickly.

Pivot away from guard.

Keep control of ball. Move quickly.

Figure 15-32

BASKETBALL RELAYS

Basketball Passing and Catching

Shuttle formation (Figure 15-33).

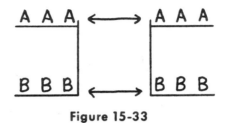

Figure 15-33

Basketball Dribbling

Shuttle formation (Figure 15-33).

Basketball—Pivoting

Shuttle formation (Figure 15-34).

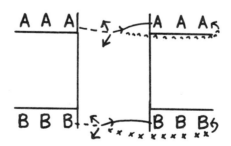

Figure 15-34

Basketball Dribbling

Circle formation
Spoke formation

Goal Shooting

Line formation—two lines of players for each basket. The first shoots from anywhere, then runs up and tries to catch the ball before it hits the ground. He shoots it back to the next player in line and goes to the end of the other line. Each basket counts two points for the shooter. Each one keeps his own score.

Guarding, Running and Dodging, and Shooting

Double shuttle formation—two lines of players, who are going to attack, start at the foul shooting line; the other two lines of players, who are going to guard, start behind the goal line. The two attacking leaders go at once, passing a ball back and forth to each other; the two defending guards come up toward them, and each one guards one.

Other Ball Handling Relays (Figure 15-35)

Line formation-Over Relay—pass the ball overhead, everyone touching it two hands, to the end of the line. When the last one gets it, he dribbles it to the front of the line and passes it over his head.

Under Relay—pass the ball between the legs, rolling it on the ground. If it goes out, the one responsible for it goes after it and shoots it under his own legs when he gets back with it.

Over and Under Relay—the first player passes the ball over his head; the second one between his legs, etc. When the last one in

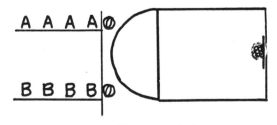

Figure 15-35

line gets it, he dribbles it to the front of the line and passes it over his head.

Goal Shooting Relays—any of the above, plus shooting once for the basket.

BASKETBALL LEAD-UP GAMES

Seven or Bust

Line up in two teams, facing the basket (or pole goal). The first player on each team shoots from anywhere he wants to, recovers his ball, and shoots again from there. If his first shot goes in it counts two; if his second shot goes in it counts one, whether the first shot went in or not. Then he shoots the ball to the next one in line, and goes to the end of the other line. When he makes exactly seven points, he wins the game. If he makes more than seven, he busts, and must start all over again.

Twenty-One

Similar to Seven or Bust, but played as a team game, so the players stay on their own team. The team first making exactly twenty-one points wins the game.

Teacher Ball

Played passing the ball.

Ten Pass Keep-Away

Played passing the ball.

Pass and Change

Form a large circle of six to eight players, each player having a number, with one player in the center with the ball. He calls two numbers and then says "Go." They must exchange places, and then go back to their own places while he throws the ball to a third player who throws it back to him. Then, he tries to hit one of the runners, as in Dodge Ball. If he does so, he stays as "It"; if not, the player that first got back to his original place becomes "It."

Captain Ball

Have the playing area divided by a center line and marked by circles about four feet in diameter and four or five feet apart (Figure 15-36). Each team consists of three guards, on one side of the center line, each one guarding a captain from the opposite team; and three captains, on the other side of the center line, each one in a captain's circle. Each captain must keep one foot inside his circle at all times. The game starts by one of the guards having the ball, and trying to pass it either to one of his captains, or to another guard on his team. The object of the game is to throw the ball from one captain to another on the same team, thus making two points. The guards try to keep the opposite captains from doing this. Fouls are: a captain steps both feet out of his circle at once; a guard steps into a captain's circle; holding the ball more than three seconds; taking more than one step holding the ball; or hitting the ball out of someone's hands. The penalty for any of these fouls is that the other team gets the ball. Have the players referee themselves, and just hand the ball over to the one against them if they foul. Play ten minute halves.

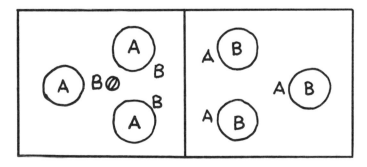

Figure 15-36

Foul Shooting Drill

Have a team of four to six players at each basket. Number one stands just behind the foul-shooting line while the others line up on each side of the "Key," ready to jump for rebounds (see Figure 15-37). Number one shoots a foul shot. If he makes it, he shoots again. He continues until he misses, each shot going in counting one point. All rotate, and number two shoots, and so on. See who gets the most points each turn around.

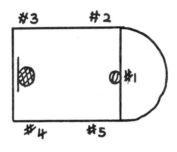

Figure 15-37

Spot Shooting

Have two teams of four to six players at each basket, lined up on a diagonal behind number one (Figure 15-38). Number one

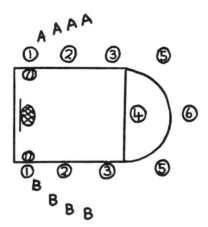

Figure 15-38

from both teams shoots from number one spot. If he makes it, he shoots from number two spot, and so on. If he misses, he goes to the end of his team. Next time it is his turn, he shoots from wherever he got to before. Each basket that goes in counts two points. See who first gets a shot in from the last spot.

Circle Basketball or
Circle Pole-Goal Basketball

Similar to Circle Pin Soccer, but played throwing and dribbling the ball trying to make baskets either through a basketball basket or through a pole-goal. It is a foul to take more than one step holding the ball, to hold the ball more than three seconds, or to hit it out of someone's hands. The penalty is that the other side gets the ball. The leader throws the ball in so that it bounces first to one side, and the next time to the other side. The outside circle of players stop the ball with their hands and throw it in to somebody on their own team.

One-Basket Basketball or
One Pole-Goal Basketball

Combine the game of Ten Pass Keep-Away, without counting the passes, with shooting for baskets. Each basket made counts two points. Start the game by tossing the ball up between two players for a jump ball. After each basket it is given to the other team, on the end line, near the basket. Try to keep the game open; keep away from each other; do not bunch together.

Six-Man Basketball

Similar to Six-Man Soccer but played passing and dribbling a basketball, using the rules given under the other basketball games.

Volleyball

Fundamental Skills of Volleyball.

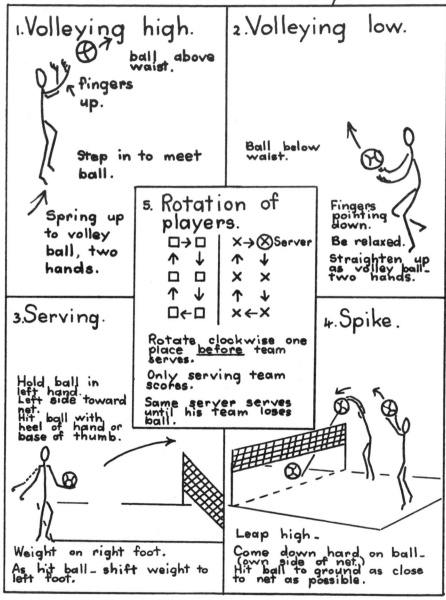

1. Volleying high.

ball above waist.

fingers up.

Step in to meet ball.

Spring up to volley ball, two hands.

2. Volleying low.

Ball below waist.

Fingers pointing down.

Be relaxed.

Straighten up as volley ball_ two hands.

5. Rotation of players.

□→□   X→⊗Server
↑   ↓   ↑   ↓
□   □   X   X
↑   ↓   ↑   ↓
□←□   X←X

Rotate clockwise one place **before** team serves.

Only serving team scores.

Same server serves until his team loses ball.

3. Serving.

Hold ball in left hand.
Left side toward net.
Hit ball with heel of hand or base of thumb.

Weight on right foot.
As hit ball_ shift weight to left foot.

4. Spike.

Leap high_

Come down hard on ball_ (own side of net.)
Hit ball to ground as close to net as possible.

Figure 15-39

VOLLEYBALL RELAYS

Volleying High

Double shuttle formation—the first one from each line steps ahead, and the four players volley high back and forth to each other. Then they go to the end of the opposite line.

Volleying Low

Double shuttle formation—the first one from each line steps ahead, and the four players volley low back and forth to each other. Then they go to the end of the opposite line. Then try volleying high and low with a net.

Volleyball Serving

Have two rows of players, one on each side of the net, three or four yards away from the net. The first player on the right has two chances to serve the ball over the net. The right hand receiver tries to volley it back, and the two continue until the ball is dead. Then they go to the end of the opposite line.

Volleyball Spiking

Have two rows of players, one on each side of the net, about two yards away from the net. The receiving side moves up closer to the net. The first player on the right of the "serving" side sets the ball up to himself, close to the net, and then attempts to spike it. The receiving side tries to send it back. When the ball is dead, the first player from each side goes to the end of the opposite line.

VOLLEYBALL LEAD-UP GAMES

Volleyball Skill Relays

The volleyball skill relays could be done in groups of six to eight players as games, both sides rotating whenever the ball is dead. They could all be done either with or without a net.

Volleyball Twenty-One, Rotating

This is best done in groups of six to eight, although it can be done in larger groups. All the players are on the same team, half on each side of the net, well spread out. One player serves the ball; then all try to volley it back and forth twenty-one times over the net without having it hit the ground, go out of bounds, or go under the net. Whenever it does one of these things, both teams rotate one space clockwise, somebody else serves the ball, and start counting all over again. Both teams should have a forward and a back row of players.

Volleyball Modified

Have six-man teams, with three in the forward line and three in the back line. The back right hand corner player serves first, trying to get the ball over the net. One player may assist him by hitting the ball too. The server may have two chances to get the ball over the net, in bounds. Once served, the ball is volleyed back and forth over the net until it hits the ground, goes out of bounds, or goes under the net. It counts a point for the serving side if it hits the ground in bounds on the receiving side, or if the receiving side fails to return it in bounds to the serving side. The server keeps serving until his side loses the ball. Then, the other side rotates and becomes the serving side. Only the side serving may make points, and only the team just becoming the serving team rotates. If a serve hits the net and goes over the net, in bounds, it is called a "Let" ball, and the server has an extra serve; if a ball is volleyed into the net and goes over the net, in bounds, it is still in play.

In learning the game, it is well to let the server serve only two points. If his side still has the serve, the serving side rotates and the next player continues with the serve.

Play the game in ten minute halves, or until one side reaches either fifteen or twenty-one points.

Softball

Fundamental Skills of Softball.

1. Throwing overhand.

Weight changes to left foot.

Weight on right foot.

Right shoulder back - bring arm up and back. close to ear. Throw straight ahead, follow through with opposite leg.

2. Catching.

Keep eyes on ball.

To catch a fly ball. Keep in line with ball.

Fingers up - hands cupped. Wrists close together. "Give" as ball hits hands.

To field a grounder. Get body behind hands - fingers down. Feet close together.

Grasp ball tightly.

Always keep eyes on ball.

5. Pitching. (underhand.)

Swing right arm back.

Weight on left foot.

Swing right arm back. As arm comes forward step on left foot and pitch about hip high.

3. Batting.

Keep eyes on ball.

drop bat.

Weight right foot.

Weight left foot

Follow through

Weight right foot. Weight left foot

Arms away from sides. Bat parallel to ground. (Bat - Trade mark up.)

4. Base running.

1st. base.

Run!

After hit ball - drop bat and run FAST to 1st base.

Figure 15-40

SOFTBALL RELAYS

Throwing and Catching

Shuttle formation. Throw overhand.

Pitching

Line formation, with one player as the catcher. After a player pitches, he becomes the catcher and the old catcher brings the ball back to the next one in line and then goes to the back of the line. Pitch underhand. Pitch at a block to knock it down, through the back of a chair, or directly to the catcher, between his knees and shoulders. Aim. Count a point every time the pitch is a strike.

Base Running

The runner makes a home run, being sure to tag each base with his foot as he goes by it. He runs against the second hand of a watch. If there are two diamonds of the same size near each other, two runners could go against each other, one on each diamond.

SOFTBALL LEAD-UP GAMES

Peppers

This is batting practice. Have six players on a team, arranged with a catcher, a batter, and the other four in a more or less straight line between third base and first base. The player nearest the pitching position pitches the ball, underhand, to the batter, so that he can hit it. He tries to hit it directly to one of the four in line facing him. He makes as many hits as he can in three pitches, and then all players rotate clockwise one space. Each player keeps his own score. It is a good idea to try to hit any pitch and to hit gently.

Teacher Ball

This is another good formation for throwing and catching, and pitching practice.

Scrub

This is best played in teams of six to eight. Arrange the players with a pitcher, batter, catcher, third baseman, second baseman, and first baseman. This is also the simple rotation order. If there are eight players, have a short stop-fielder between third and second, and another one between second and first. If there should be nine players, add a center fielder. Each player is for himself. After a batter makes a fair hit he runs to first base and back to home plate, thus making a point for himself. After three hits, if he isn't put out before, everyone rotates clockwise one position.

He may be put out by getting three strikes on himself, by the fielding players getting the ball to first base before he gets there, by them getting the ball to home plate if he is between first and home, by a player catching a fly ball, or by a player tagging him out.

Beat the Ball Scrub

This game is similar to "Scrub" except that the batter tries to make a home run once he hits a fair ball. Unless a fly ball is caught, the fielders throw the ball to first baseman, no matter where the runner is, who throws it to second baseman, who throws it to third baseman, who throws it to the catcher on home plate. If the ball beats the runner home, the runner is out. If the runner beats the ball home, he is safe, and makes himself one point. Then all rotate.

Beat the Ball

This game is similar to "Beat the Ball Scrub" except that

there are two teams, one in the field and one up to bat. When everyone on the batting team has been up once, the fielding team comes up to bat. When all players have been up once it is an inning. Five innings make a good game.

Softball Modified

This is best played in teams of six to nine players each. Have a home plate and three bases, anywhere from thirty to forty-five feet apart, depending upon the size and skill of the players. One team is in the field; the other team is up to bat. Bat in rotation. Pitch the ball underhand.

When the batter hits a fair ball (in the playing area, somewhere between first and third base lines or their extensions) he runs to first base, or farther if he can. Once he stops on a base he stays there without taking a lead off the base until the next fairly hit ball. A run is scored when the runner gets back to home plate safely.

The runner is out if: the ball gets to first base before he does; a fly ball is caught; or he is tagged by a player with the ball in his hand when he is off a base. A batter is out if he has three strikes, or if a foul tip is caught on strike three. Children often play that four fouls put them out, in order to keep the game moving quickly. When there are three outs, the other team comes up to bat. If there is an umpire, a strike is called, whether the batter swings at it or not, if the ball goes over home plate between the batter's knees and shoulders; a ball is any pitched ball that is not a strike. A foul hit is a strike except on the third strike, when it gives the batter another chance. If there is an umpire, four balls walk a player to first base. When both sides have had three outs, an inning is called. Seven innings usually make up a game. When the players are more experienced, they may try to steal a base once the ball leaves the pitcher's hands on a pitch.

EVALUATION

For the Children

Do I know, understand, and stick to the rules of the game? Can I make up a new game something like this one—or maybe correlate it with some other subject?

Do I play safely, with no rough-housing? Am I having fun playing? Are others having fun, too?

Do the children like me when it is my turn to be the captain? Do they like me as a team member?

Can I take winning or losing with good grace? Will I keep playing hard until the end of the game?

Am I able to explain the game to others, as at home after school?

Am I gaining in skill in the game? Am I gaining in coordination—in endurance—in team work?

For the Teacher

Can I explain the main points of the game very quickly so that the children can get started to play? Then, do I remember to call them together so that we can all discuss how the game went, and so that I can explain some of the finer points to them?

Can I get the children to think of ways of making teams fairly? Can I get them to see that close games are far more exciting than games where one team is way ahead of the other? Can I get them to see that the way to do this is to have all teams as nearly equal as possible in both physical and mental ability?

Can I really let the children settle their own difficulties unless they ask me for help? Can I let them do a lot of the talking?

Can I get the children to play hard, to stick to it, to take turns at things—to want to play fairly and to want to be good sports? Can I get them to see that they have more fun this way than they would have otherwise?

PART FIVE

Rhythms

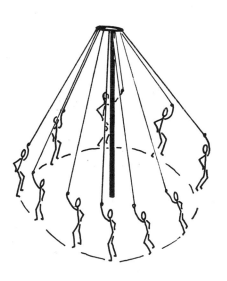

16

Rhythmic Activities

Rhythms include activities done in time with music, to a beat, or to count, either alone, or as a member of a group; each one either doing his own activity, working out things in a small group, or all doing the same thing, each in his own way. Rhythms include movement exploration (helping the child to think as he moves in rhythm, mimetics and story plays, chants and rhythmical games, ball bouncing and dribbling, rope jumping and swinging); rhythmic physical fitness exercises; singing games, folk dances and square dances.

Rhythms are fun; they can be used as an outlet for emotions; they help to build up endurance, and therefore are a part of physical fitness; they are strenuous; and they come naturally to many children.

OBJECTIVES

Movement exploration includes many types of activities wherein all may move at once, trying to use all possible space, trying to keep clear of all other children and things so that there are no collisions. It may be used in all parts of physical education. Try it.

In "Helping the Child to Think as He Moves in Rhythm" the child is finding out some activities that his body can do, and is learning to keep his balance. In further exploring movement and

207

space in mimetics and story plays, chants and rhythmical games, he is acting out things, in his own way. He is learning high and low, up and down, around and around. He is learning how much room he takes in doing things, and how much space different things take. His imagination has free play, as long as he bothers nobody else, and keeps in time with some beat or musical rhythm. He learns more about keeping time by clapping or tapping the rhythm as he moves; by ball bouncing and dribbling; and by rope jumping and swinging.

In singing games, folk dances and square dances, the child is developing a sense of belonging to a group. He is learning how to be at ease in his social relationships with other children. He is finding out that he is worth-while not only to himself but also to the entire group. These activities correlate nicely with social studies and reading. They are vigorous activities, and the child must be thinking clearly and quickly in order to keep up with the music.

METHODS

Be sure that the child knows what he is going to do. Give him time to think it out. Be sure that he understands he must not bump into anyone else. Be sure that he understands that he must move in time with the music. Have the children listen to the music, or the drumbeat, or the count. Have them try to feel the rhythm by clapping or tapping it and also by singing it.

Have plenty of room. If there are any hazards in the room, be sure that all know what and where they are, and why they are hazards. Ask each child to try to keep control of his body at all times. One method of doing this is to take short steps. Another possible method would be to start off a few at a time until all are moving.

In singing games, folk dances and square dances, listen to the instructions and the music. Briefly explain each step and have them walk through them. Try to see how the actions fit with the music. Try to feel the rhythm. After going through the steps with the music repeat any explanations necessary. Then do the entire thing again. As soon as possible do with joy and vigor many times. Sometimes challenge them: "Can you do this one through the record again without puffing?"

Change partners often. Let the children help each other learn the steps. Ask them to be very light on their feet. Sometimes over-accent the accented notes. Stress doing each step well, with no rough-housing. Also stress good manners, thus getting in good boy-girl relationships.

Most rhythm records have the instructions either on one side of the record, or on the cover of the record or album. Use them. They will save the teacher a lot of talking, and they will also help the children to listen carefully, as directions are usually only said once.

17

Movement Exploration

Movement exploration helps each child to feel important. For many of the activities there is no right nor wrong way—there is only the child's way. The child must think about what he is trying to do, and then be able to do it in his own way. In the meantime he is also a member of a group, so he must watch his own space. He is doing these activities to music, and must conform to the rhythm. There is much thinking involved along with much action.

Start by establishing a rhythm or beat. Have the class follow the teacher's instructions with the different rhythms, clapping softly with the fingers into the palm of the opposite hand; or tapping the rhythm with the toes of one foot; first in place, and then using all the space in the room. For music use a phonograph record or a tape with a strong rhythm, drumbeats, blocks or rhythm sticks. Try a single clap per beat; a single clap per measure; double claps per measure; combinations; and various accents. Can the children think up different rhythms?

HELPING THE CHILD TO THINK AS HE MOVES (K-3)

If there is enough equipment, divide the children into groups so that several have a turn at once. Have three or four children demonstrate the activity and then give all a chance to try it. Once the children understand what they are to do, have them try it in rhythm, which is much harder than just doing it, as they must listen and think very hard. In the two sections called "Finding Out Some Activities That His Body Can Do" and "Learning to Keep His Balance" the child really has to think as he moves. Be very careful in the rope or line hopping, the walking board and the low balance beam, and the stepping stones. In this type of movement exploration the child is developing coordination and courage. Some will need the security of teacher's hand in order to even try. Giving the child assurance that taking short steps is the correct way also helps.

Once the activities are learned and thoroughly understood, have different activities going on in various parts of the gym, with a student leader in charge of each group of two or three children. Let them move freely from one activity to another, as a group. Use all the space in the room. This involves much thinking, since they plan where to go next and learn how to be good sports and wait for their turns. The teacher will be very busy at first helping where a child needs help, helping the little groups move from one thing to another, and probably helping the children to decide how they should act as they move.

All of these activities help the children learn how to find themselves in space. They help them to try to coordinate the various parts of their body, to try to follow directions, to develop their courage, and to be careful in their movement exploration that they do not bother others in any way.

HELPING THE CHILD TO THINK AS HE MOVES IN RHYTHM

Finding Out Some Activities That His Body Can Do

A drum beat is especially good for these. Be sure that he thinks hard!

Obstacle Course (Figure 17-1)

Place a board or yardstick across two chair seats. Step over it without touching it.

Figure 17-1

Put the board or yardstick across the backs of two chairs. Duck under it without touching it.

Place two chairs back to back, close enough so that the child must turn his body sideways in order to get through. Squeeze through without touching it.

Angels in the Snow (Figure 17-2)

Have the children lie on their backs on the floor, arms at sides and feet together. Have them move their arms along the floor, up behind their heads until their hands touch each other—then back to position. Have them move their feet wide apart, keeping their heels on the floor—then back to position.

Then have them move just their right arms up and back; or their left arms; then their right legs, or left, apart and back; then right arms and left legs, or opposite. Continue giving various directions.

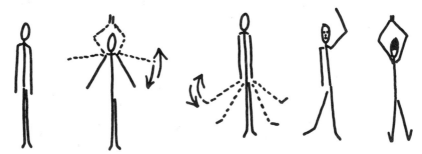

Figure 17-2

Change time; move quickly; move slowly; try various ways, as face down instead of on backs.

Creeping

Move along on hands and knees, arms and legs in opposition (Figure 17-3).

Figure 17-3   **Figure 17-4**

Crawling

Move along on stomach, arms and legs in opposition (Figure 17-4).

Learning to Keep His Balance

Rope Hopping, or Line Hopping

Each child has a jump rope which he stretches out straight on the floor. (Or the children can use chalk lines or lines on the floor.) Starting at one end of the rope, each child hops back and forth over it to the other end, both feet together, going frontwards; then going sideways; then going backwards (Figure 17-5).

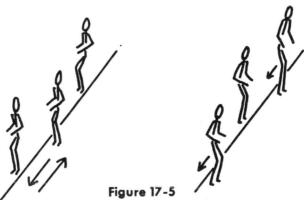

Figure 17-5

Same, hopping right foot only; left foot only; alternating feet; twice on each foot; twice on one foot and once on the other.

Can the children make up other ways of rope hopping?

Walking Board or Low Balance Beam

Have several boards 2 inches by 6 inches, 8-10 feet long. Use some of them flat on the floor, as boards; set the others into low standards for use as low balance beams.

Walk forward, taking short steps, keeping good posture, eyes fixed on some point straight ahead, at eye level; then walk sideways; then backwards (Figure 17-6).

Try walking forward part way, then turning-or bouncing-or doing some exercise, as a deep knee bend, or a flying angel; then continue walking to the end (Figure 17-7).

Can the children make up other ways?

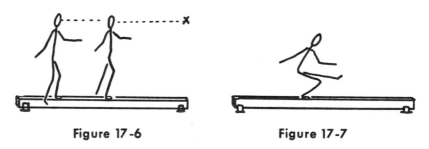

Figure 17-6   Figure 17-7

Stepping Stones

Have 20 or more 10-12 inch squares of cardboard, half each of two colors—as 10 red and 10 green ones. Each child must step on the red squares with his left foot only; and on the green ones with only his right foot.

Arrange the squares on the floor, alternating colors, and at irregular distances apart, so that the child is required to take steps of different lengths and in different directions. He may even have to cross his feet, one over the other. Try to go the whole distance without making a mistake (see Figure 17-8).

How can the squares be arranged for this activity? How else?

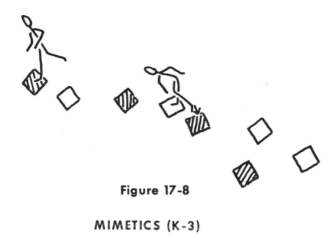

Figure 17-8

MIMETICS (K-3)

These are all "make believe" activities, done in rhythm with some kind of music—hand clapping, toe tapping, drum beat, piano music, phonograph record or tape recording. Mimetics usually lead from doing or being something to acting out nursery rhymes or songs; and acting out nursery rhymes or songs usually lead into acting out story plays.

The child acts out doing or being the thing—or the nursery rhyme or song, or the story play—sometimes alone, sometimes with a partner, and sometimes as a member of a group of children. The greater their imagination the more they can usually do with this kind of movement exploration, and the more they enjoy it.

They must remember to keep control of themselves at all times, not to bother anyone else, and to keep in time with the rhythm. The larger they can make their actions the more exercise they get in doing these things. Use all possible space.

These activities can also be used as guessing games, done either individually, with a partner, or as a group. Have the others raise their hands and guess what is being done when they are called on. After three wrong guesses, tell them. In acting out these things as a group, the entire group could act out each part, or different members of the group could act out different parts in order. Could different members of the group act out different parts all at the same time? What would the results be?

Acting Out Doing or Being Anything

Keep in rhythm with some kind of music—such as hand clapping, a drum beat, a phonograph record, or a tape recording.

Examples

1—Chinning
2—Bouncing balls (Figure 17-9)
3—Rag dolls
4—Airplanes
5—Windmills
6—Pulling a rope (Figure 17-10)
7—Splitting wood
8—Cross-cut sawing
9—Digging a hole

Figure 17-9

10—Pop corn
11—Rowing a boat (Figure 17-11)
12—Raking leaves
13—Climbing a ladder
14—Shovelling snow (Figure 17-12)
15—Automobiles
16—Trains
17—Can you think of others?

Figure 17-10

Figure 17-11

Figure 17-12

Acting Out Nursery Rhymes or Songs

Chant or sing the words. Suit the action to the words.

Examples

1—Jack Be Nimble (Figure 17-13)
2—Little Jack Horner
3—Jack and Jill
4—See Saw, Marjorie Daw
5—Swinging in a swing
6—Hickory, dickory dock
7—Bow-wow-wow
8—Where, oh where has
   my little dog gone? (Figure 17-14)
9—Little Sally Waters
10—Pussy cat, pussy cat
11—Ten Little Indians (Figure 17-15)
12—Sing a song of sixpence
13—Three times around went
   the gallant ship
14—Can you think of others?

Figure 17-13

Figure 17-14

Figure 17-15

STORY PLAYS (K-3)

As a class, make up a story about something, together. Have the children divide into groups. Have different groups act out different parts of the whole. The next step would be to have each group act out each part of the whole, in sequence. The teacher could play appropriate music for the story, and ask the children to try to act with the music. Or, he could ask each group of children to make up a story and act it out, and have the others guess what they are doing.

Examples of Story Plays

1—Going to school
   As: Be a pupil—a teacher—be re-
        cess—be a book
2—Going on a picnic
   As: Be a game—a car—be a camp-
        fire—a storm
3—Thanksgiving (see Figure 17-16) (A)
   As: Be the food—thankful (B)—be
        the afternoon—
        good-bye (C)
4—Christmas
   As: Be a tree—the spirit
        of Christmas—
        decorations
5—Abraham Lincoln
   As: Be the boy studying
        by candle-light—
        Honest Abe—the
        feeling for the
        people

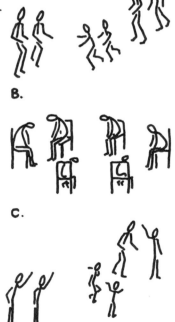

A.

B.

C.

Figure 17-16

CHANTS AND RHYTHMICAL GAMES

Mimetics, doing or being something, nursery rhymes and songs, and story plays usually lead right into chants and rhythmical games. Remember to keep a rhythm going in all of these activities. Make up the action to many of the chants—just suit the action to the words. This is movement exploration too. Also, have the children make up the chants. Once they learn them, children like to do them again and again.

Magic carpet and musical chairs are two games done with music that everybody enjoys. Be sure to keep in rhythm.

While all of these activities can be done by the entire room at once, they are even more fun to do in groups of six to eight because there are more "Its" or more winners. Be sure that all have plenty of room and that all can hear the rhythm.

CHANTS (K-3)

Suit the action to the words. Chant or sing the words.

I'm Tall; I'm Small

One player stands with his back to the others. The leader stands where all can see him.

Words:	*Action:*
"I'm tall, I'm very tall;	—All stretch up tall on tiptoes.
I'm small, I'm very small;	—All crouch way down.
Sometimes I'm tall;	
sometimes I'm small;	—Do it.
Guess what I am now."	—All do whatever the leader has done. "It" tries to guess what they are. He may be "It" as long as he is right.

Old Mother Witch

All follow "Old Mother Witch" chanting: "Old Mother Witch, fell in a ditch; picked up a penny, and thought she was rich." Then, all stop. Mother Witch asks them "Whose children are you?" All answer, "Mrs. _____'s." Then they chant and follow Old Mother Witch again. On the third time, the children answer "Yours," and she chases them back home. She pretends to stir any that she catches into her "Stew pot," and they stay in it one turn. She chooses a new Old Mother (or Father) Witch.

Three Times Around Went the Gallant Ship

Have a double circle facing center. The inside one is the ship, and goes in one direction; the outside one is the crew, and goes the opposite direction. Suit the action to the words.

> "Three times around went the gallant ship;
> Three times around went she.
> Three times around went the gallant ship,
> Then she *sank* to the *bottom* of the *sea.*"
>
> "Pull her up, pull her up," cried the brave sailor boy;
> "Pull her up, pull her up," cried he.
> "Pull her up, pull her up," cried the brave sailor boy;
> But she *sank* to the *bottom* of the *sea.*
>
> "Then along came a captain big and strong,
> With a great big anchor and chain.
> And he threw them down to that gallant ship,
> And pulled her up again."

Swinging in the Swing

In groups of three, suit the action to the words.

> "Swinging in the swing; swinging up so high;
> You can almost bump your head, up against the sky."

RHYTHMICAL GAMES (K-6)

Magic Carpet

Three or four "Carpets" are drawn on the floor, about six feet long, and three feet wide. Sometimes it helps if a line, or "Sidewalk" is drawn from one carpet to another to show the way. All players march (or walk, or skip, or hop) in line, going right over the carpets, being careful not to touch each other. On a signal, or when the music stops, all stop immediately. Any caught on a carpet must drop out. See who stays in the game the longest. Instead of being out of the game when caught on a carpet, all could keep playing, and see who never gets caught at all.

Musical Chairs

Arrange chairs in a long line, every other one facing in the opposite direction. There should be one less chair than there are players. On a signal, all start marching around the chairs, not touching them. Stand tall. On the next signal, or when the music stops, all try to get a seat. They must get into the chairs from the front. The one left out must drop out. Take a chair away each time. See who can stay in the game the longest. Instead of a long line of chairs, this may be played in several groups, each group of players going around a set of chairs.

BALL BOUNCING AND DRIBBLING (K-6)

Try different sized balls, letting the children choose the size they want, with a ball for each child if possible. Try to have them get the rhythm by just making believe; bounce or dribble at first as teacher gives the instructions. Then try to get the rhythm using the ball. They must keep their eyes on the ball, and try to coordinate fast enough to keep up with the music. If a child misses and the ball gets away from him, he must try to get it without bothering anyone else. This will all take a lot of practice, as exploring movement and space is quite different with a moving ball from what it was just alone or with a stationary object.

Stand with the feet slightly apart, knees slightly bent, holding the ball in both hands, about waist high, watching the ball. Drop ball and catch it as it bounces back up. When a child gets good at this, have him push it a little as he drops it. Try doing it keeping in time with music, making it hit the ground on the accented beat. Have the child say the rhythm as he does it: as, "Bounce catch three four—bounce catch three four;" "Bounce catch-bounce catch;" or "Bouncy bouncy bouncy catch." (See Ruth Evans Childhood Rhythm Records—Series 2.) Can the children work out different rhythms using one ball for each two people? Can they work out rhythms to fit other music?

In ball dribbling, instead of catching the ball after each bounce, keep pushing it back down, using the finger tips (finger tip control,) fingers spread, keeping the ball low, bouncing it between knee and waist high. Keep in time with the music, trying to do the following things:

1) Dribble the ball in place, first watching it and then looking ahead.
2) Try walking forward, backward, and sideways dribbling it.
3) Try going around in a circle, making the circle larger and larger. Keep head up, watching where there is enough space.
4) Can the children work out patterns using these ball dribbling rhythms?
5) Can the children work out patterns using one ball for each two people?

(For music, Ed Durlacher's Honor Your Partner Album #12 is very good.)

ROPE JUMPING AND SWINGING (K-6)

Each child has a rope about six feet long. (It should be long enough so that he can hold it one end in each hand shoulder high, with the center of the rope just touching the floor.) First try jumping; then swinging; then cowboy jumping. (Here, too, Ed Durlacher's Honor Your Partner Album #12 is very good.) Get the rhythm of the music and try to keep in time with it.

For jumping, keeping his elbows close to his sides and his hands out, he swings the rope by rotating his wrists so that the rope goes down and under him as he jumps, then back, up and forward.

For swinging, he holds both ends of the rope in one hand, puts the back of his other hand on his hip, and swings the rope double—over his head parallel to the floor, or left or right side. Keep in time with the music.

Cowboy jumping is holding the rope as for rope swinging, bending forward, rotating the wrist first toward the body, swinging the rope just above floor level, jumping each time it comes near his feet. At first, try jumping first one foot and then the other; then try both feet at once.

Besides jumping the rope, the child may try running over it as he swings it, skipping, crossing his arms as he jumps, or jumping backward. Try jumping one leg, or with a stiff knee, or "spread eagle" jumping with the feet apart.

Then combine ways and try to make patterns, jumping part of the time and swinging part of it. The children will need to work on their coordination especially, but once they get it, will build up a lot of endurance.

For fun, see how many times the child can jump in half a minute, or in one minute. See how long it takes him to jump fifty times or one hundred times.

EVALUATION

For the Children

Can I move with the beat? Can I feel the rhythm? If I lose the rhythm, can I get back in with it?

Is my imagination working well? Can I get the feeling of how whatever I am trying to show would act and feel, and act and feel accordingly? Am I getting less self-conscious?

Can I keep both myself and a ball in rhythm at the same time? Can I keep in rhythm with a jump rope? Can I make up patterns to try with a ball or a jump rope?

In exploring movement and space am I getting a better understanding of where I fit in? When I am in a group, do I have good ideas, and can I express them so that my group can try them out?

Am I gaining in self-confidence and poise? Can I keep my emotions under control? Can I really let myself go in time with the music and yet not get silly nor rambunctious?

For the Teacher

Do I have the children clap or tap the rhythm before they start to move? Do I accent the beat well to help them get the rhythm?

Do I let the children use their own imaginations in doing movement exploration? Can I manage not to always tell them how I would do it? Can I help them to keep from copying each other?

Do I give the children enough time to think about what they are going to do? Do I give them enough chances to create their own rhythmical activities?

Can I sense where I am needed most in a class? Can I be at the right place at the right time? Do I have them use all possible space?

Do the children enjoy movement exploration? Do I give them enough time so that they can really build up their endurance? Do I remember to remind them to always watch out for each other's safety?

18

Singing Games, Folk Dances and Square Dances

Singing games are games put to music, with words, one verse usually leading to the next. Folk dances come from various countries and may or may not have words. Square dances are American folk dances. The basic square dance calls will prove to be very helpful in teaching square dances, and should be taught as needed.

The progressive lists of singing games and folk dances for grades K-3 help the teacher to see where what he is teaching fits in with all the rest of what the child has had before and what he will be having later. The lists of folk dances and square dances especially suited for grades 4-6 correlate very well with their social studies and reading. All singing games, folk dances and square dances listed here have been tried many times and found to be very popular with the children. Each one has its own character and rhythm and is quite different from the others. Some of them can be used as seasonal or holiday rhythms just as they are; some of the others can be easily adapted to the various holidays. Have fun doing them!

The suggested rhythm records and albums have all been proved to be of great value in teaching rhythms. The ones listed here all have a very strong rhythm, and are the right speed for elementary boys and girls. A record player with a variable speed control would be most helpful in teaching rhythms.

Teach the singing games, folk dances and square dances to the entire class at once. Have them listen to the music and clap or tap—or both—the rhythm, softly. Say the words and have them repeat them, and then fit the action to the words. Go slowly at first and then try at proper speed. Talk through-walk through is a good approach. Have the class sing the words as they do the action. If there are no words, try singing the action to the music; such as "Slide together, slide together, step, step, step," or "Skipperty, skipperty, skipperty—!" The children usually think that made up words are lots of fun! There is good carry-over value if the children can get the words, the tune, and the action all fitted together.

If the directions are given on the record, get the class into the proper formation before starting the record. Have them listen to the directions as they clap or tap the rhythm. Then have them go through the action as the record gives the directions.

Have fun. Keep the feet light. Listen carefully. Keep thinking. Keep the body under control. Have good manners. Use the singing games, folk dances and square dances so much that the children know which one is which when the music is played, and can get into the right formation and start doing the dance by themselves. Change partners often, and teach the children to be partners gladly with anyone in the class. Try to have all feel wanted in the group.

One more big hint: If the record is played fairly softly, the class is apt to be quieter than it would be if the record were booming at them!

SOME BASIC SQUARE DANCE CALLS

In American square dancing, keep something moving all the time, in time with the music, as clapping hands softly, or tapping the toes of one foot to the floor. The step is a graceful, gliding walk. Often children like to skip instead.

A square is made up of four couples, the girl on the right of the boy. Couples #1 and #3 are the head couples, and face each other; couples #2 and #4 are the side couples, and face each other.

Honor your partner—bow or curtsey to partner.

Honor your corner—bow or curtsey to the one on the boy's left or the girl's right.

Eight hands around or circle left—all join hands and go clockwise.

Swing your partner—similar to social dance position (facing partner, boy's right hand is at the small of the girl's back, her left hand is on his right shoulder; his left arm is gracefully out sideways, elbow bent some, and her right hand is in his left) turned slightly right, with the outside of right foot outside of partner's right foot. Pivot on right foot, pushing off eight times with the left foot, bending knee slightly on each push, and turning with partner once around clockwise.

Promenade—boys and girls like to do this standing side by side, with right hands joined, and left hands joined. It should take sixteen counts to walk once around the set counterclockwise.

Do-si-do—walk toward each other three steps, passing right shoulder to right shoulder; side step right one step, behind the other person, and go back to place in three steps.

Allemande left or *allemande your corner*—face corner. Join left hands and hold them high; walk around each other once with four steps, counterclockwise, ending where you were.

Grand right and left—face partners. Join right hands; all move forward, passing by partner, and join left hands with the next person; right to the next, and so on. Boys go counterclockwise; girls go clockwise, as you do this, you are weaving in and out or out and in.

Balance partner—face partner. In the boy's directions (Girls are just the opposite) step left foot, and swing right toe across it, touching floor; same with other foot; repeat, first one foot and then the other.

Ladies chain—in four counts, the girls opposite each other touch right hands as they go to the opposite girl's place. The boys turn the girls, by taking their left hands with their left hands, placing their right hand behind the girl's back, and turning them to face "home." Repeat, going back to place, and turning with their own partner. This can be done in either eight or sixteen counts. Usually, only the head couples or the side couples do this; when all do it at once, it is called "Ladies grand chain."

Right and left—similar to "Ladies chain," but the boys go with their partners, cutting between the opposite couples, ladies passing between the two boys. Each boy turns his own partner. All return and turn. This takes either eight or sixteen counts.

Progressive Lists of Singing Games and Folk Dances (K-3)

The following singing games and folk dances are especially suited for the grade given here. Of course there are many more, probably equally as good, but these will give the children a good foundation in rhythms.

NAME	NATIONALITY	COMPANY—Record Number
Kindergarten		
Farmer in the Dell	English	Folkraft—#1182
Here We Go Round the Mulberry Bush	English	Folkraft—#1183
Let the Feet Go Tap, Tap, Tap	German	Folkraft—#1184
Go Round and Round the Village	English	Folkraft—#1191
Did You Ever See a Lassie?	Scottish	Folkraft—#1183
Five Little Chickadees	English	Folkraft—#1184
Grade 1		
Looby Loo	English	Folkraft—#1184
Bridge of Avignon	French	Folkraft—#1191
Dance of Greeting	Danish	Folkraft—#1187
A-Hunting We Will Go	English	Folkraft—#1191
Shoemaker's Dance	Danish	Folkraft—#1187
How D'Ye Do, My Partner?	Swedish	Folkraft—#1190
Muffin Man	English	Folkraft—#1188
Rig-A-Jig-Jig	American	Folkraft—#1199
Oats, Peas, Beans	English	Folkraft—#1182
Chimes of Dunkirk	Fr.-Belgian	Folkraft—#1188
Carrousel	Swedish	Folkraft—#1183
Grade 2		
Sing a Song of Sixpence	English	Folkraft—#1180
Paw Paw Patch	American	Folkraft—#1181
Jolly is the Miller	American	Folkraft—#1192
Jingle Bells	American	Folkraft—#1080
Jump Jim Jo	American	Folkraft—#1180

Shoo Fly	American	Folkraft—#1185
Skip to My Lou	American	Folkraft—#1192
I See You	Swedish	Folkraft—#1197
Bluebird	American	Folkraft—#1180
Pease Porridge Hot (or Beans)	English	Folkraft—#1190

Grade 3

Indian Dance	American	Folkraft—#1192
Yankee Doodle	American	Folkraft—#1080
Broom Dance	German	Ruth Evans Childhood
Nigarespolska	Danish	Rhythm Records—
Donkey Dance	Mexican	Series 10
Children's Polka	German	Ruth Evans Folk
Bleking	Swedish	Dances—Album #1
Seven Steps	German	
Sailor's Hornpipe	English	Folkraft—#1329

Lists of Folk Dances and Square Dances (4-6)

These are only some of the many folk dances and square dances suitable for grades 4-6. The children like them all.

FOLK DANCES

NAME	NATIONALITY	COMPANY—*Record Number*
Bingo	American	Folkraft—#1189
Captain Jinks	American	Folkraft—#1070
Cshebogar	Hungarian	Folkraft—#1196
Seven Jumps	Danish	Victor—#6172-45
Troika	Russian	Folkraft—#1170
Irish Washerwoman (Irish Jig)	Irish	Folkraft—#6178-45
Highland Fling	Scottish	Folkraft—#1177
Minuet	French	Folkraft—#1179-45
Ace of Diamonds	Danish	⎫
Mountain March	Norwegian	⎬ J. Burns-Folk Dances—
Gustaf's Skoal	Swedish	Album B
Tarantella	Italian	⎭
Carillons de Dunkerque	Canadian	⎫
Frere Jacque	Canadian	⎬ Canadian Folk Dances—
Maple Leaf Stomp	Canadian	1-12" 33 1/3 R.P.M.
Prairie Circle	Canadian	Selected and edited
Canadian Lancers	Canadian	by Eileen Reid
Card the Wool	Canadian	⎭

La Raspa	Mexican	⎱	
La Bamba	Mexican		Mexican Folk Dances—
La Cucaracha	Mexican		1-12" 33 1/3 R.P.M.
Chihuahua	Mexican		Educational Record
Chiapenecas	Mexican		Sales-New York, N.Y.
La Jesucita	Mexican		

Square Dances

Little Brown Jug Mixer	
(or Pattycake Polka)	Folkraft—#1260
Oh Susannah (mixer)	Folkraft—#1186
Virginia Reel	Folkraft—#1249
Portland Fancy	Folkraft—#1243

Solomon Levi		
Golden Slippers		Carson Robinson Square Dances—
Spanish Cavaliers		1-12" 33 1/3 R.P.M.
Jingle Bells Square Dance		Educational Record Sales—
Paddy Dear		New York, N.Y.
Turkey in the Straw		

Susanna		
Heads and Sides		Honor Your Partner Album #1—
Honolulu Baby		Talk through-walk through
Do-Si-Do and Swing		by Ed. Durlacher
Around the Outside and Swing		

EVALUATION

For the Children

When I hear the music, do I know what singing game, folk dance or square dance goes with it? Can I start doing it? Are my feet light? Can I get the feel of the music and keep with it?

Can I accent the first count of each new step? Can I change partners at the right time without getting out of rhythm?

Do the others like to have me for their partner or in their group? Can I be happy being partners with anyone in the room? Do I feel that I belong in the group, and do I sometimes help others to feel that they belong too?

Do I have fun doing singing games, folk dances or square dances? Can I keep myself under control and yet get a lot of action in time with the music? Do I understand how important good manners are in these activities?

For the Teacher

Do I fit rhythms in with social studies or reading whenever possible to help make the people of the countries "come alive" for the children? Can I get the children to watch television shows for folk and square dancing, and report on how the people were dressed?

Do I have the children do the singing games, folk dances and square dances enough so that they can recognize the music for each one that they have had? Can they fit the proper action to the music?

Do I let the children help each other at times in learning the steps? Do I try to make them all feel both wanted and needed in the group? Can I get the children to see that good manners are essential to good folk and square dancing?

Do I make singing games, folk dances and square dances so much fun for the children that they include them in their party activities both at school and at home? Do I enjoy watching them do them? Do I ever allow them to put on a program for their parents?

Suggested Rhythm Records
and Albums

Folkraft Records (1159 Broad St., Newark, New Jersey—07114) can provide almost any singing game, folk dance or square dance (with calls) record. Instructions are either on the record folder or on a separate paper. They also have many folk dance and rhythm albums.

Educational Record Sales (157 Chambers St., New York, New York—10007) carries almost any physical fitness, movement exploration, singing game, folk or square dance record or album that a teacher would want. (All charge orders must be signed by an authorized school or library official.) If a desired record isn't listed, they will try to get it. The instructions are either on the records themselves, on the record or album folder or on separate papers. The following are suggested as excellent aids to the physical education program. Educational Record Sales has them all.

Ruth Evans—Childhood Rhythm Records (complete instructions included):
    Series 1-Fundamental rhythms-animals-toys-play-character
    Series 2-Rhythm combinations-including bouncing balls and
        jumping rope
    Series 9-Rhythm groups and combinations
    Series 10-Dances
    —Folk Dances (complete instructions for each step):

Volume 1 (Primary grades)
    Bow, Bow, Belinda-Bleking
    Children's Polka-Donkey dance
    Dan. Dance of Greeting-Seven Steps
    Chimes of Dunkirk-Carrousel
Volume 2 (Intermediate grades)
    Put Your Little Foot-Kolo
    Oh, Susanna-Csebogar
    Heel and Toe Polka-Swedish Clap Dance
    Corsican Dance-Parts 1 and 2

J. Burns—Folk Dance Albums (instructions on records):

Album A (Primary grades)
    Lassie Dance-Minuet
    Dutch Couples-Swiss May Dance
    Good Night Ladies-Tantoli
    Come, Let Us Be Joyful-Shoemaker's Dance
Album B (Intermediate grades)
    Tarantella-Highland Schottische
    Csardas-Ace of Diamonds
    Dan. Crested Hen-Nor. Mountain March
    Gustaf's Skoal-Irish Lilt
Album E (Grades 3-6)
    Little Dutch Girl-Nixie Polka
    Hi, Little Lassie-Tropanka
    Hansel and Gretel-Paw, Paw Patch
    Indian Dance-Martin Wappu

Olga Kubitsky of Hunter College (Instructions for each dance):

Folk Dances, Song Plays, Play Parties-
    (Primary grades)-single records
Folk Dances and Mixers-(Intermediate grades)
    single records

Canadian Folk Dances (with instructions—edited by Eileen Reid) See list for grades 4-6.

Mexican Folk Dances (easy-to-follow instructions) See list for grades 4-6.

Carson Robinson Square Dances (called by Lawrence Loy) See list for grades 4-6.

Ed Durlacher's Honor Your Partner Albums, with "Talk through-walk through" instructions and calls, plus a manual with instructions and figures. (Some have "See "n" do" instructions.)

Album 1—Square dances-(See list for grades 4-6)
Album 12—Rope skipping-(Ball Bouncing)
Album 14—Physical Fitness Activities-Primary
Album 15—Physical Fitness Activities-Intermediate
Album 25—Postural Improvement
Album 20– Holiday Dances
    Wearing of the Green-Witches Shack
    Jingle Bells-Turkey in the Oven
    Easter Parade—Maypole Dance
    Georgia Camptown Meeting (Patriotic)

Physical Fitness Awards

Send to the following addresses for information about the: American Association for Health, Physical Education and Recreation Physical Fitness Standard or Merit Emblems and tests:

AAHPER
NEA Publications-Sales
1201 16th St. N.W.
Washington, D.C. 20036

They also have Special Fitness Awards for the Mentally Retarded and Special Awards for the Physically Handicapped.

The Presidential Physical Fitness Award address is:

President's Council on Physical Fitness
Washington, D.C. 20201

Selected Bibliography

"Teaching Physical Education in Elementary Schools"
    Vannier, Maryhelen and Mildred Foster
    W. B. Saunders Co., Philadelphia, Pa.   1963

"Methods and Materials in Elementary Physical Education"
    Jones, Edwina; Edna Morgan and Gladys Stevens
    World Book Co., Yonkers-on-Hudson, N.Y.   1957

"Teaching Physical Education in the Elementary School"
    Salt, Benton; G. Fox and B.K. Stevens
    Ronald Press, New York, N.Y.   1960

"Physical Education for Elementary Schools"
    Neilson, N.P.; and Winifred VanHagen
    The Ronald Press, New York, N.Y.   1958

"Physical Education for Elementary School Children"
    Ruth Evans
    McGraw-Hill Book Co., New York, N.Y.   1958

"Complete Book of Games and Stunts"
    Darwin A. Hindman
    Prentice-Hall, Inc., Englewood Cliffs, N.J.   1956

"Youth Fitness Tests"-AAHPER and The President's Council
on Physical Fitness
    NEA Publications-Sales, Washington, D.C.   1965

"Royal Canadian Air Force Exercise Plans for Physical Fitness"
    Revised U.S.A. Edition, Canada   1962

"A Developmental Program"
    Halsey, Elizabeth and Lorena Porter
    Holt, Rinehart and Winston, Inc., New York, N.Y.   1963

"Physical Education in the Elementary School Curriculum"
    Miller, Arthur G. and Virginia Whitcomb
    Prentice-Hall, Inc., Englewood Cliffs, N.J.
    3rd. edition, 1969

"How We Do It Game Book"
    AAHPER
    Washington, D.C.   Rev. Ed. 1964

"Becoming Physically Educated in the Elementary School"
    Charles Corbin
    Lea and Febiger, Philadelphia, Pa.   1969

Index